KILL
JIMMY
COCHRAN

The True Story
of the St. Louis
Metropolitan Police
Department's plot
to assasinate
serial bank robber,
and abductor,
James Leroy Cochran

To: Charlie Brennan
From: James Jelly Roll Cochran
314-954-3033

Timothy C. Richards

KILL JIMMY COCHRAN

© 2020 by Timothy Charles Richards

ISBN: 978-1-63110-477-0

Printed in the United States of America

Published by xznark Press LLC
St. Louis, Missouri 63129

xznark.com

Acknowledgements

My friend Charlie Brown at the Mercantile Library for assisting me with the research needed for this book, and the other five nonfiction books about old city cops and old city crooks.

My friend, Chief Neil Kurlander, (Maryland Heights Police Department, retired, and St. Louis City Police Department, retired), and friend, Lieutenant George Venegoni, St. Louis Metropolitan Police Department, retired.

My mom, Marjorie E. Richards, who recognized early in my life that I would probably have a tough time conforming to the discipline needed to succeed in life. She taught me to read, write and type at an early age; before second grade. She was a High School English teacher and she lovingly took me step by step through the process of forming thoughts and putting them on paper.

Thanks, mom!

Author's note

This is a work of nonfiction. Research materials included police reports, news archives, interviews, and some victim statement material.

The author uses true names, places, and dates, and he has endeavored to maintain the factual and quintessential integrity of both the people and the events related herein.

1

St. Louis is a strange little city. It sits alone in the Great State of Missouri, down by the Mississippi River, a rifle shot across the nasty Mississippi River from the infamous burg of East St. Louis, Illinois. The State of Missouri is thriving to the west of St. Louis. Lake of the Ozarks is a prime example of the state's beauty, and it is known throughout the world as the place to be during the summer months. Nobody in Illinois gives a damn what happens in East St. Louis, Illinois. Missouri (outstate) feels the same way about St. Louis.

The City of St. Louis split from St. Louis County in 1879, a divorce that was probably fueled by liberalism within city politics. St. Louis prides itself with liberal ideology. But that left the city vulnerable to experimentation by the federal government.

The city had a huge populace of southern blacks, dependent on welfare and seeking jobs. The local politicians didn't desire to bring these folks into the work force. Unions didn't want to hire them, and politicians most always go with the flow of the unions in and around St. Louis, Missouri.

So, with the assistance of the federal government, huge housing projects were built by the trade unions, paid for by the feds, and everybody got rich off of the idea and felt lucky to be in this racist little socialistic/democratic town down by the Mississippi River, divorced from the county and shunned by the state.

The welfare checks rolled in every month, and the food stamps, and the free health care and education, and any other freebie one could think of from everybody's favorite uncle. The blacks existed on subsistence, drove junky cars, did odd jobs if they could find someone to hire them, and were hated by the white establishment for being poor, and for being black, and for having their own language, and for dressing differently. The blacks hated back, and still do, even though white folk in St. Louis have reached leniency. But it's too late.

An amazing wonder drug was introduced to the black community in the 1950s, by the Chicago Mafia (the only true Mafia institution, started by Al Capone and still in existence) in most democratic controlled cities in America; Heroin! For the weak day trippers, living in high rise projects with their grandmothers and their numerous offspring, heroin was a death trap.

But for the entrepreneur, the black ghetto inhabitant who was offended by the government handouts and the imprisonment of projects, and food stamps, and always being broke, heroin was the stepping-stone to wealth, if he or she could stay alive.

St. Louis, and cities like St. Louis, were being portrayed in movies about black men fighting the heroin wars, and most were getting killed. Art imitates life. Hollywood always tossed in a crooked federal politician, and a couple of crooked cops, but it was about as real as one could imagine from the perspective of the cop on the street.

In 1970, this cop/writer became a City of St. Louis cop, and was assigned to the bloody ninth police district, the Central West End district. It was a cool place, and the cops who were assigned there loved it. On the west end of the district, the homes off of Euclid Avenue, were movie star glamorous. They were, and are architectural works of art. Hortense Place, a gated street is where Elsa

Lemp, (Lemp Brewery heiress) was murdered in 1920. It was ruled a suicide, money talks, bullshit walks. Nothing ever changes in the United States Judicial System.

Congressman Bill Clay was the United States House Representative for the first congressional district. Many ninth district cops had been in his presence time and again because Bill Clay frequented the bloody ninth district. He would observe cops during their assignments, whether it was a peace disturbance or a homicide. He never interfered; he intelligently observed. St. Louis cops were at times detached to Bill's public speeches and heard him speak numerous times.

He was articulate, educated and smooth, unlike his constituents. It was unusual how he was always elected by the slum dwelling, project living welfare folks; except for his light color, (the slum dwellers referred to his color as "high-yella"), he was a polar opposite. They elected him every two years from 1969 through 2001.

During Bill Clay's tenure as the federal leader of the first congressional district, the heroin trade flourished. Fat Woods was the premier heroin dealer to the city. He was a fat black man who lived in and around the Pruitt Igoe Federal Housing Project.

The local chapter of the Italian Mafia gave Fat Woods heroin on consignment, and he sold it. He was successful because he hardly ever got "stiffed" by his dealers. If the money got funny, it meant sudden death by the Italians.

Sam Petty, Joe Petty and his brother Lorenzo, were leading a close second to Fat Woods in the area's "kill a black man with dope" club. Lorenzo owned a neighborhood confectionary near the Walnut Park District, which was at one-time-working-class-white, until the feds initiated the 235 loan, which enabled black folks to buy homes for almost nothing and only make the payments when they wanted to.

The Walnut Park neighborhood had cute and immaculate brick homes, shadowed by the massive Bellefontaine Cemetery where the beer barons and war heroes from the civil war are buried. As is usually the case, the whites fled whenever the blacks moved in; the tax base from working and caring citizens disappeared, also.

Fat Woods was incarcerated in 1973, and a Walnut Park resident, Dennis Haymon, took over his business. Haymon and the Petty brothers went to war shortly after the transition. It was a brutal war. The Petty brothers were brutal killers. They would torture and even drown their victims. Dennis Haymon was a machine gun killer.

Haymon, and the Petty brothers, were eventually incarcerated for manslaughter and other connected crimes pertaining to the drug war. All of them were released after short sentences. Lorenzo Petty was arrested again in 1978, for being a felon in possession of a firearm; an off-duty cop recognized him at a firing range, shooting a pistol. He was incarcerated for the charge: fifteen years federal time.

Joe Petty was killed in a motorcycle accident in 1984. In 1985, Intelligence Unit detectives raided Sam's house. A small amount of cocaine (enough for personal use) 10,000 rounds of ammunition, bullet proof vests, and several guns were confiscated. Sam was arrested for being a felon in possession of a firearm, another federal offense.

Sam's ex-wife was subpoenaed to testify before a federal grand jury. She was shot and killed in broad day light as she got into to her car to go to the courthouse.

Sam Petty went away for another federal vacation, got out, relocated to Atlanta, and died. Dennis Haymon is allegedly now a preacher. Lorenzo is out and tells youngsters in the "hood" to stay away from the "gangsta" lifestyle. Words falling on deaf ears.

Coincidentally, the Chicago Mafia had taken control of Laborers Local #42, and #110, predominantly white unions. They also controlled Pipefitters Local #562. All of these powerful union organizations were headed by thugs; they gave money generously to the democratic politicians. None of the democratic leaders in the St. Louis region ever publicly addressed the black heroin business, or the fact that the Chicago Outfit controlled organized labor in St. Louis.

But, when Lieutenant Colonel John Doherty assigned his hitmen, Sergeant Glen Lodl and Detective Rich Kuklajon, to intercept a vehicle connected with an abduction of a police officer, and to eliminate the driver, who they thought was the crook, instead of a city police officer, (Patrolman Steve Georgeff), who they shot and almost killed before realizing they had shot the wrong man, Congressman Bill Clay called for a Grand Jury investigation, and a Congressional inquiry. Neither occurred. (Detailed in the nonfiction book, Superman's Eyes.)

Bill Clay's son, Lacy Clay, took his dad's place in the political arena of the First Congressional District. It's funny how that happens. Lacy Clay now got reelected every two years. Whenever Lacy Clay speaks, the casual observer can't help but think that he might have been adopted. But the poor blacks, demanding their entitlements from the fed, elect whoever is running on the

Democratic ticket. If a black Republican ran, he wouldn't stand a chance. The white union organizers demand a Democratic vote and the black politicians demand the Democratic vote. St. Louis is politically screwed.

A single mom, protest leader, nurse, and black woman, ran against Lacy Clay. She won! For some unknown reason, liberals in America feel that the future of the country lies on the backs of single black women. Lacy Clay knew how to play the game of politics in old corrupt St. Louis; "do what the union leaders tell you to do". It will be interesting to see how Cori Bush handles the pressure.

St. Louis is still carrying the dubious distinction of being the murder capital of America. Ninety percent black, shooters and victims. The politicians blame the mass murder on drugs. Drug usage and dealing has some bearing on the problem, but the main reason is ignorance. Anyone in Missouri can carry a gun, legally, if you are not a convicted felon or under the age of twenty-one.

Ignorant people don't fight, anymore, they shoot. If someone says something derogatory about someone else, the word travels through these African American neighborhoods like jungle drums. It is survival of the smartest and fittest, or who can kill first. Most of the killings go unsolved.

The local clergyman in the city were upset about the young blacks being slaughtered. Lacy Clay was always seen in the background with a concerned look on his face. When it was his turn to give his spiel, he blamed the violence on the present administration in Washington D.C. Of course, it is a Republican Administration.

2

From 1966 through 1977, the demographics of the City of St. Louis changed drastically. The fed owned St. Louis, from the Arch to Skinker Boulevard. Without the fed, the city would collapse. The tallest and newest building in the downtown section is the Federal Courthouse. Coming from the West on Clayton Avenue, the courthouse blocks out most of the Arch. It's almost as if the Fed is throwing its power over us in our faces. The fed was steering ghetto, housing project blacks into the neighborhoods of north St. Louis. The pristine neighborhood around the Calvary Cemetery (Walnut Park), West Florissant and Riverview Boulevard were targeted, but the residents didn't know it.

St. Louisans were accustomed to high-rise federal housing projects, the type surrounding the downtown district. These projects were deemed a failure by the fed. The tax-dollars spent to build them was wasted. The local union organized criminals reaped the reward from those gigantic construction fiascos, and the projects were eventually razed.

The Walnut Park residents felt they were safe from federal housing because they had the Calvary Cemetery in their midst, and there was nowhere to build any high-rises, or low-income houses. But the fed wasn't looking for land to build; the fed wanted their cute little well cared for homes, and they got them.

Lombardo's Restaurant had been situated at the corner of West Florissant and Riverview Boulevard for three decades. It was a first-class establishment, modern and nice looking. The three brothers who owned it, Gus,

Angelo, and Carmen, felt secure that they would be able to stay at their location. Calvary Cemetery gave them false hope. They purchased the movie theater situated behind the restaurant and had it razed so that they could have a buffer, if and when the neighborhood changed.

The best laid plans of mice and men. St. Louis is a federal town. The fed determines what gets built, and where the masses live, and there is nothing anyone can do but follow the fed's plans. The neighborhood around the restaurant went black.

White diners would experience black pedestrians spitting on their table side windows while they were eating dinner. Customers stopped going to Lombardo's. The brothers sold the building for pennies on the dollar and opened several restaurants around St. Louis.

The entire north St. Louis corridor changed demographically in a couple of years. The inhabitants of Walnut Park fled to Spanish Lake, an unincorporated north St. Louis County municipality which had new ranch style homes and first-class apartments with swimming pools and tennis courts. It was resort style living for pennies, and the folks who fled Walnut Park, and who went into the fancy apartments, had money in the bank for the first time in their lives. All working-class people have, usually, is their homes. They live paycheck to paycheck, just like the welfare recipients.

At about this same time frame, (early to mid-70s) there was an international oil crisis. The gigantic art treasure houses in the Central West End, referred to as CWE, and the West End of the city were being abandoned. Most had oil burning boilers to heat, more than one for each house. Even the wealthy aristocrats opted out of those houses.

The ghetto directly north of the CWE was close enough to the art treasures that the street of Euclid, now fairly much abandoned, became the pathway for burglars to plunder anything of value from these historic properties.

There were empty storefronts on Euclid, and an entrepreneur (Pete Rothschild) purchased a building at the south east corner of Euclid and McPherson and began purchasing old clothing, or fireplace mantels, or anything he surmised might be of value to someone. It was a secondhand store and it made Pete Rothschild wealthy, even though he came from wealth.

Pete was and is a super salesman. He's mush-mouthed and he speaks like a European nobleman. It isn't an act, it's just his personality leaking out of his psyche. He continued to purchase real estate on Euclid, and eventually purchased a home for himself and his family on the most sought-after street in the CWE, Hortense Place. He became the prince of Euclid.

The cornerstone of the CWE was Gaslight Square. It had a ten-year run of success, from the early 60s until the early 70s. Black criminals killed Gaslight Square. It was the supreme entertainment district in St. Louis. Street life, good restaurants, good entertainment, swing bands, girls in gilded cages dancing their hearts out for almost no pay. It was sad to watch it deteriorate. It made old St. Louis young again. Every evening at Gaslight Square was like an evening at the 1904 World's Fair.

As businesses began closing on the square, the underworld crept in; it became the dope and prostitution neighborhood of the city. Heroin was sold on the street, in houses, and in loft apartments. Street hookers walked the streets day and night.

The cops knew the hookers, pimps and dope dealers by name, and they knew us. We were all prisoners of circumstance, locked into our lifestyle because we had nowhere else to go, and had nothing to lose. It was a symbiotic relationship.

In the harsh St. Louis winters, some of the cops would allow the street hookers to get into their police cars to get warm. The girls would talk, but they would never talk about their pimps; that meant death. They all had imaginary children they were working to feed, or some such extravagant tale. Sick parents, disabled husbands, it was gibberish. They worked the streets to get enough money (after paying their pimps) to purchase heroin. Like most of us cops; they were lost souls.

Being in the presence of lowlife scum, like pimps, the street cop wants to hate them, beat them, and end their lives. But the pimps are cunning, like snakes. Some have the ability to recognize, in some of the cops, a certain understanding of the game of cop, pimp, trick and whore.

It is a simple business equation; The pimp has something to sell. Some people wish to purchase it. He is the middleman, and he offers the protection that wayward women need and want in the plying of their trade. Some cops identified with the pimps, and some became friendly with them.

A cop, Michael Paul, came to the bloody ninth district in the summer of 1976. By then, Gaslight Square was just a lingering dream. The streets were bare, and the once glitzy restaurants, and nightclubs, were shuttered.

Mike was a police academy acquaintance. We had laughed and drunk beer together for the four months of training. Both veterans, Mike was a combat survivor from

Viet Nam. The St. Louis Metropolitan Police Department searched for guys like us.

Mike went to the fifth police district; white ghetto, close to the Mississippi River, railyards, and heavy industry, and he had a couple of other assignments before being assigned to the ninth. It was a place he always wanted to come to.

He loved it, like most of us. The ninth had everything. In Mike's mind, patrolling in the bloody ninth district was a continuation of his time in Viet Nam, in combat in la drang Valley. Only the appearance of the enemy had changed.

On the night in question, Mike was driving his scout car west on Olive toward Sarah. Sarah and Olive was the biggest pimp, whore, heroin, corner in the Midwest. There were ghetto hotels on the corners, and scummy bars inside of them. Lowlifes who were never accepted in Gaslight Square now frequented Sarah and Olive. Anyone was accepted there, if they had cash.

Mike spied a pimp (most were easy to spot because of their Caddy's or Lincolns) so Mike activated his red lights and pulled the pimp over. Maybe this particular pimp thought he knew Mike. He didn't try to conceal his pistol. It was lying on the floor next to him. It was a nice gun, a Browning, Hi-Power 9-MM.

Mike arrested him. The pimp went to the hospital after Mike pistol whipped him for trying to attack him, and eventually warrants were issued, and it was a federal case due to the pimp being a felon in possession of a weapon. That usually means a five-year gig in the federal vacation system.

Time rolled on. The pimp arrest was just another incident for the cop to dwell on. Nobody else in the judicial system cared about it, until the trial date comes around, then the cop has to speak with the United States Attorney, and some other folks who do everything in their power to make the cop think they actually like him, which they don't.

So, it was getting close to trial time for the big pimp arrest, and Mike was doing what every cop does in this situation; he ponders. Mike was on an alarm sounding call and his assisting officer was an older, seasoned ninth district cop. He and Mike gossiped and laughed about the cop business, and the assisting cop brought up the arrest by Mike of the pimp with the federal gun case looming.

Mike listened as the older cop droned on. Mike knew his assisting officer was friendly with a lot of the street people in the district; thieves, pimps, whores, drug dealers, and in general low-life scum that cops deal with on a daily basis.

The bottom line: the cop offered Mike $10,000 to poison the case against the pimp. Mike asked him how much he was getting out of the transaction. He stated, "$3,000." Mike went to court; the pimp got five years.

Mike was hired by the Naval Investigative Service (NCIS) in May of 1981 and departed good old St. Louis. St. Louis had been his home for his entire life. In 1989, Mike was hired by the Defense Intelligence Agency, and a year later he was hired by the Central Intelligence Agency. When he was fifty-nine years of age he served as Director of Intelligence for the Multi-National Security Transition Command-Iraq. He then worked as a civilian Department of Defense contractor as a counter-narcotics advisor, and a police advisor in Afghanistan from 2008-2013. He is retired and lives in the Great State of Kentucky. He still misses the bloody ninth district.

3

The bloody ninth continued to deteriorate, and so did
the city. The once vibrant downtown was becoming
dangerous. It wasn't safe to park your car and walk to the
many large department stores. Northwest Plaza in St.
Ann, St. Louis County, opened and it was a big draw
from downtown St. Louis. Parking was free and people
felt safe.

The once successful street of Lindell (connecting west
St. Louis with Olive street east) was losing its glamour.
It, at one time, had a Playboy Club many good restaurants
and nightclubs. People weren't coming to the CWE for
anything but hookers, and heroin.

As Gaslight was in death throes, the few remaining
bars (a hippie bar, a gay bar and a soul bar) eventually
closed. The owners of the empty businesses were
desperate to make money, so they rented out the upper
floors of their now defunct nightclubs to anyone who
could afford the rent.

There were groups of hippie types coming and going
in the old square. One apartment might hold ten or so
inhabitants on one day, and then have only one or two the
following day. It was free love, sex, drugs and party time.
I never could figure out where they got the money for this
lifestyle; none of them worked.

The ninth district cops (mostly country and/or ex-
military) hated the commune second floor dwellers. They
were never a problem for this cop. Tolerance, within
reason, is the key to dealing with unstable people.
Although most of the district cops had been on dangerous

peace disturbance calls at some of the apartments, which is no big deal. It is what cops do most, try to keep the peace. In fact, in the State of Missouri law enforcement officers are referred to as, peace officers.

There was one big oaf of a guy, Paul Stearns. He was big and thick, and he had brown hair combed straight back and it went down to his shoulders. He was dangerous in appearance and his demeanor. His body language was aggressive.

Naturally, the country, ex-military cops targeted Paul Stearns. He was arrested frequently, for anything the cop could think of at the time, and Paul had a big mouth: which meant he got his ass kicked by the PO-lice often.

If a cop observed Paul Sterns walking down the street, on the sidewalk, in the front of his goofy hippie crash pad apartment, the cop would inadvertently stop and verbally attack him. It was mostly because of his hair. And Paul, not being very bright, would tell the cop to go fuck himself, which always ended in a fight, which Paul would lose because two or three cops with nightsticks almost always win. The turnkeys at the prisoner processing division were on a first name basis with Paul Stearns.

Calls for disturbances continued at the hippie crash pad at 4324 Olive. As usual, Paul Stearns was always there, but the faces of the other occupants changed every time we went there. There was a noted new face, a guy we arrested for possession of weed. The kid's name was Richard Rau, and he grew up in an upper middle-class home in Kirkwood. His parents cared for him, but he was hooked on illegal substances, so he ended up living with Paul Stearns in the hippie crash pad.

Richard Rau, (Ricky) came to our attention regularly, and he was arrested regularly by bloody ninth district officers. He looked to Paul Stearns for protection; they were buddies in a place where there were none.

A visitor to the crash pad, George Lipscomb, became agitated at Ricky Rau; Ricky was apparently making fun of him for some reason. George didn't play that, so he stabbed Ricky to death. Cop/writer got the call, and George Lipscomb was arrested. He was gang raped in the city jail by a group of black prisoners. At least that's the story Paul Stearns frequently told with an addendum; George Lipscomb committed suicide, in jail.

Paul Stearns moved out of the Gaslight Square district, to north St. Louis County, with a young girl who had lived with him on Olive. Paul stayed out of the city, at least the bloody ninth district. Then he lived on Folsom, in south city after the north county residency. He kept a low profile. Paul always had cute, young hippie girls around him.

This cop's good fortune continued with a transfer to the Intelligence Unit in 1978. The socialist newspaper ran a story about Paul. He had killed a Tampa, Florida cop, in north St. Louis County, at a party near the Municipality of St. John. The Tampa cop, Terry J. Bergmann, was honored as Tampa officer of the year in 1977, and he had visited the St. Louis area to meet with relatives who lived here. A relative invited him to the party, and in attendance was Paul Stearns, cop hater supreme.

Someone at the party was in possession of a .357 magnum pistol, and Paul somehow came into contact with the gun and had it in his possession. Terry Bergmann asked Paul to stop playing with the weapon, and he and Paul began scuffling on the back porch of the residence. It was 4:15 a.m. and the party had been going on for twelve hours.

The scuffling went to the floor of the porch, and from witness accounts, Paul placed the weapon at Bergmann's face and pulled the trigger. End of Officer Bergmann. Paul left the scene and hired an attorney. He turned himself in with his attorney at his side. He was indicted for second degree murder. Paul made bond.

Mysteriously, a witness for the prosecution to the incident concerning Paul Stearns and Terry Bergman, was killed in an automobile accident. Robert Welch was at the party when Paul killed Terry Bergman. He observed Paul Sterns point the magnum at Officer Bergmann's face and pull the trigger. Paul's defense was that it was an accidental shooting.

The accident that killed the key witness, Robert Welch, occurred when he was a passenger in a van driven by Edward H. Schults, a friend of Paul Stearns. They were driving home from a boating party when Schults asked Welch to go to the rear of the van and get him a beer out of a cooler. Apparently, the sliding door of the van was open, and Schults inadvertently turned the van and Welch went out of the cargo door and was killed.

The Tampa cop case went to trial, and Paul Stearns testified in his own defense. He was subsequently convicted of manslaughter and sentenced to ten years in the state penitentiary. There's a moral to this story; none of us should be where we don't belong, especially cops.

There were no businesses left on Gaslight Square. The ornate gaslight street lamps were still there, but there was no gas hooked up to them. Slowly, one by one they disappeared. The dope, hooker business, thrived. At times there would be thirty hookers walking and waving at cars. In the summer they would wear revealing clothing and bare their breasts at passing cars.

There were times when the Captain, Harry Lee, would order us to arrest them. We would call for a paddy wagon and then chase them down like fleeing geese; none of them could run very far, they were stoned on heroin, or going through withdrawal. When they ran their breasts would flop out of their clothing and flap up and down like summer cantaloupe. It was cop/hooker comedy at its best.

 We would forcibly place them into the paddy wagon while they were berating us. They knew the street cops; we all had name tags bearing our last name. A new order came down from headquarters; any time a prisoner is placed in a paddy wagon, a district officer had to ride in the back with them. We all rode in the back with twenty or so hookers many times.

They didn't hate us; they knew we hardly ever hassled them. "Why you doing this to us, Richards?" they would ask. "I'm not doing it to you, I'm locked up back here with you."

They would calm down, until we got them to the station and booked them for prostitution. We took their property, which meant their wigs. Many refused to remove their wigs. We'd snatch them off of their heads and stick them in their property bags. They would do twenty hours in the police holdover, get out, and the day after their release they would be back on the black girl stroll in Gaslight Square, Olive to Washington and back again. It was a joke.

It was a joke because in order to make a prosecutable case for prostitution, an undercover detective acting as a John would have to be propositioned by the prostitute. The city didn't have the time or the money for that, so we "flopped" them just to get them off of the street for a day or so. It was just something to do.

So, the Vice Division devised a scheme: Since the prostitutes knew most of the district cops, on sight, who were assigned to the bloody ninth district, the headquarters leaders would place out of district cops into the stroll area and wait for them to be propositioned by the local pimps or hookers. They called it a prostitution detail, and they asked for volunteers from some south city detective bureaus.

Apparently Detective Gregory Erson, family man, clean cut, good cop and good man, was chosen. It was a warm summer night. The decoy just has to sit in a decoy (funny) car at a lot at Whittier and Westminster Place and wait to be approached.

Detective Erson had made six arrests for prostitution on that fateful evening. He was shot while sitting in his car and he died inside of the decoy cop car. Local pimps, or street walking hookers didn't murder Detective Erson. Two wandering armed robbers, intent on robbing a white John observed him, approached him and shot him. They stole his wallet, his badge and his gun. Both were ultimately captured and received life sentences. One of them was murdered in prison.

A vice cop, Detective Gregory Chase, had worked the detail for years. He had had similar experiences. Robbers jump inside of the decoy cars intent on killing. First, they want you to give them your wallet, jewelry, and any other thing that's of value, then they murder you, because you are white. Vice Detective Gregory Chase, a bloody ninth district alumni, had sent many of the robbers to the stroll in hell.

The murder of Gregory Erson didn't slow down the pimps and hookers. They were out in force the very next day, plying their trade. They were entitled; it was their right as Americans to sell sex. The law was on their side. Allegedly, the world's oldest profession.

The heroin dealers were as bad as the pimps and whores. They would stand on Olive, in the 4200 block, usually next to a gangway they could use for an escape route in case they needed to run. But there was a catch 22 in the dope game in old Gaslight Square. Some of the dealers were being robbed, and some were being shot after or during the robbery.

The heroin dealers who survived the shootings told investigating officers that it was a white cop who shot and robbed them. All of this information was kept on the down-low within the bloody ninth district, but the Homicide Section, and Internal Affairs was working the theory.

Nothing is secret for very long in the St. Louis Metropolitan police Department. Supervisors in the stroll area advised their offices that if they see any white, off duty cops, lurking around the area to advise them immediately.

The theory was that the alleged cop, dressed in civilian attire, ballcap to hide his face, would drive a few blocks from the Gaslight Square area, park his car and walk down to the stroll and heroin sales market, possibly walking in alleys.

The gangways that were used by the heroin dealers backed to alleys; it's how the dealers escaped from the cops and other heroin dealing competitors. It's a rough way to make a living. The theory has it that the off-duty cop would sneak up behind them from the alley, via the gangway, and rob them. If needed, he would shoot them.

Apparently, the alleged cop/robber/shooter, robbed often throughout the city. Gaslight Square wasn't the only whore, heroin dealer location within the boundaries of the City of St. Louis. So, the secret got out, and the robberies and shootings slowed down, and the alleged cop was never arrested.

Sergeant John Siebenman, our supervisor was asked about the theory. "There's approximately 2,000 cops in the City of St. Louis; then you've got about three hundred City of St. Louis Sheriff's deputies, and no telling how many security guards. You think they're all righteous?"

4

St. Louis names its neighborhoods. It's almost like "what high school did you go to?" The way folks from St. Louis rate you on the spiritual and economical totem pole of life. If you attended a high-class parochial school, that meant your parents were well off, or had inherited money, or were maybe professional people, and that you might someday, be a professional person.

If you were a guy, talking to a strange girl, at a parochial school event, and you advised her you went to Vianney, and she went to Holy Cross, then she would probably be interested in you as a possible candidate for romance.

The Baden neighborhood was connected to the Walnut Park neighborhood. If one would draw a line, N.E. from Lombardo's Restaurant, directly across the 314 acres of Calvary Cemetery, and then across the 470 acres of Bellefontaine Cemetery, you would hit the German and Irish Catholic neighborhood of Baden. The residents of Baden, like the Walnut Park residents, also had the false sense of protection given to them by the cemeteries.

A lot of city cops came from the Baden neighborhood: Sergeant John J. Johnson, a cop union board member grew up there. John was, and is, a rational being; intelligent and fair minded. He is pragmatic to a fault.

A beautiful girl, Lisa Castrogiovanni, grew up in Baden. Like many attractive girls who grow up on the northside, Lisa had poor relationships which resulted in two children. Lisa was game and spunky. She took any job she could get to support herself and her children.

Eventually she landed a job as a summons server. She made good money, but was injured in an auto accident and had to give up the life of a private eye.

Lisa knew several cops, and she eventually married a police sergeant, who is now retired, and they live in west St. Louis County in a huge house. Lisa survived because of her moxie and intelligence.

Chief of Police for the City of St. Louis, Robert Scheetz, grew up in Baden. Bob was intense to the extent of insanity. It's what the police department desires of its members, and peer pressure is a bitch, even today. The department demands your life, and Bob Scheetz gave it to them.

There were employment opportunities in the light industry along Hall Street, and along the Mississippi River barge companies, but they were corrupt union jobs, more dangerous than being a city cop. The city cop job was actually a good job.

Of all of the colorful characters who came out of the northside neighborhood of Baden, Greg Tuck is the most notable. In Northwest High School, where he wrestled at 119 pounds, his intensity grew. He loved the competition, and he loved winning more than almost anything.

Greg was boisterous and threatening, and a winner, but was small in stature. He knew he would have to make up for his small size in a different way; he worked on his body and his wrestling; he wanted to be the best at everything he did, so he trained day and night, graduated from Northwest High School, and received a full scholarship to Southern Illinois University.

Greg studied and wrestled at SIU, and eventually opened a gym in the north St. Louis County town of Dellwood; he called it Physique World, and he was successful at the trade of helping people build their bodies beyond belief. Greg sold that gym and opened another bigger and better gym, Ultimate Gym, in the more stable city of Hazelwood, although still in north St. Louis County, and targeted by the fed for blight.

Greg was gaining a huge reputation as a street fighter. Back in the 1980's, 90's and into the early 2000's people still fought with their fists and their muscles. Greg had both, and he was about 175 pounds at that time, solid muscle, large hands and fists, and wrestling moves that few intoxicated bar flies could combat against.

Large, obnoxious, bullying criminals (police characters) frequented the bars in the City of St. Louis. It was their country club, their escape, a place where they could drink with their sycophants and be bullies.

Greg frequented these establishments. He hated large obnoxious bullies, and he was cocky and sure of himself. If confronted by a bar bully, Greg's line was, "You want to go outside and settle this?" The bully, thinking he would have someone smaller than him to beat on, would be the first one to leave the safety of the bar. Greg would stroll outside, confident and excited.

Greg's routine was simple, get the large creep off of his feet, tie him up with wrestler's moves, and pummel him with his large fists. Greg was a natural street fighter, and he always won.

The Intelligence Unit (of which this writer was a member) delighted in the tales of Greg Tuck beating up some professional criminal at a bar in the city, or north St. Louis County. He beat up many, and when some of the detectives would get into trouble with the bosses over some minor infraction (some of the detectives were snitches for the higher-ranking cops), the common saying was, "So, what are they going to do to me, get Greg Tuck to kick my ass?"

In the early 1990's, when physical training and expertise ruled in the bars of St. Louis, (now it's the puke with the gun rule), Greg's reputation had grown to gigantic proportions. People weren't seeking him to fight him (nobody wants to get his ass kicked by someone smaller than he), badass criminals were in fear of him, and trying to avoid him.

While assigned to the Drug Enforcement Task Force, (DEA), in the mid 80's, there were names being tossed around our unit on a daily basis. Criminals are snitches, and most would inform on their mother's or brothers without hesitation if it meant a lighter sentence for them.

As a rule of thumb, when we would interview a suspect and give him, or her, the opportunity to help themselves with a case they were wrapped in, some of our guys would shoot names out to them to see if they could go to them and buy dope.

We had names of possible dope smugglers, and pushers, mostly from anonymous telephone calls. North St. Louis County was targeted by DEA and other agencies; it was still mostly white, but rapidly changing.

The agent would go down the list, spouting out names, and mostly the suspect would shake his head in the negative as if he did not know them. As a last resort, the agent would say, "Greg Tuck, can you do him?" It was always a fishing expedition.

There would be a look of fear in the suspects eyes, "No, I would never do Greg Tuck."

A nasty divorce was looming, so Greg headed for San Francisco in 1993, worked at a gym there and taught wrestling at a local school. In 1995, he won the Masters

National Body Building Championship, held each year in
Pittsburgh, Pennsylvania.

Through a casual female friend, he was introduced to a
wealthy Mexican tycoon, Javier A. Burillo, whose full
name is Javier Burillo Azcarraga, a wealthy property
developer known for lavish hotels and restaurants
throughout Mexico. The Azcarraga family founded
Grupo Televisa SA, a media empire that produces
Spanish-language television programming seen across
Latin America and dominates news coverage in Mexico.

After viewing Greg's resume, and interviewing him,
he hired Greg to manage his gym in Cabo San Lucas. It
wasn't long in the employ of Javier Burillo, that Greg
became full time armed-security for Javier's children.
The cartels in Mexico were watching Javier and he feared
a kidnaping, or worse.

Javier moved his family (his wife, at that time period,
was the daughter of the late Mexican President Miguel
Aleman) to the San Francisco, California area. As early
as 1989, Javier owned Casa de Campo, a resort and
restaurant in Cuernavaca, and the Hotel Ritz in Acapulco.

Greg came back to America with them. Javier
purchased a $10.2 million bay front home in the
community of Belvedere, and then spent another $3-
million to upgrade it. Greg got an apartment several miles
away. He was still security, but while in the United
States, he was not armed. Greg watched Javier's children
grow up. They referred to him as Uncle Greg, and they
trusted him.

Javier had enough money to do whatever he wished,
so he purchased a boat, and he joined the Corinthian
Yacht Club near his mansion overlooking San Francisco
Bay. He didn't purchase a lavish boat, he just wanted to

get out onto the bay with his sons and experience the scenery and to enjoy the sea. He purchased a military style assault boat, (a 33-foot Targa Protector inflatable) the kind the United States Coast Guard, or the Marine Corps uses to drive onto beaches. Hard bottomed, rubber inflatables around it, flexible in high seas, with two powerful outboard motors.

Greg had been on the boat numerous times. Javier's sons would sit up front, near the bow. His eleven-year-old son would sit on the bow, going up and down with the swelling seas in the dangerous waters of San Francisco Bay, the big rubber and steel boat flexing with the swells.

Greg warned Javier that it was dangerous for the eleven-year-old to be siting so near the bow of the boat, but Javier didn't listen to him. The boys enjoyed being with their dad, and Greg, on the boat in paradise. But every day and everyplace was paradise for Javier Burillo and his sons.

On September 15, 2019, Javier and his two sons were boating in the bay. Both boys were sitting up front; the eleven-year-old was sitting on the bow. Javier steered the boat into a swell, which turned out to be deeper than he anticipated, the boat took a sudden rise with the wave and both of Javier's sons went overboard.

The eleven-year-old son went under the boat and was sucked back toward the propellers; he was decapitated by the props. The twenty-seven-year-old was seriously slashed in the leg by the props. Javier pulled both boys from the sea and headed for his yacht club. The eleven-year-old boy was pronounced dead at the docks of the yacht club.

The twenty-seven-year-old was rushed to the hospital in critical condition. He survived; Javier, several hours later, was arrested at his home and charged with manslaughter, child endangerment, and drunken driving. He was booked and released on a one-million-dollar bond.

Before this tragic incident, Greg was having second thoughts about his friendship with the Burillo family. He told me that Javier Burillo paid him $4,000 a month to guard him and his family members. That amount was not worth all of the heartaches and sadness associated with Javier.

He said Javier was a billionaire, but was cheap. When they travelled together, Javier wanted Greg at his beck and call during the daylight hours, but when bed-time came around, Greg had to find his own lodgings.

Greg had been employed by, and had been friends with Javier for 25-years. Greg decided to start inching himself away from Javier and his tumultuous life, and he was back in St. Louis when the boating accident occurred. "Had I been in San Francisco instead of St. Louis, I would have been on the boat with them," Greg said.

Greg chastised Javier and told him he didn't want to see him again. He quit the billionaire and headed back to St. Louis for good. He now works as a personal trainer for Wildhorse Gym in fashionable west St. Louis County.

Greg is 65-years old, still in shape, and still dangerous to the unsuspecting police character. St. Louis bullies beware.

Back to not so fashionable Baden:

The houses weren't cute brick bungalows like the ones in Walnut Park, but they were well kept, and Baden had a retail area on North Broadway consisting of almost anything one would want or desire, nice restaurants, shops, auto repair shops and a Chevy dealer. All of this was within walking distance from the Baden residents., and North Broadway connected with Bellefontaine Road, north, leading to beautiful Spanish Lake, (soon to be targeted by the fed and blighted) another unincorporated burg in north St. Louis County, a place where most north city dwellers wished to live.

Also, Bellefontaine Road is near Riverview Gardens, (targeted) working class blue collar white Irish inhabitants. A kid, Jimmy Cochran, grew up in Riverview Gardens. There were always a lot of crooks in Riverview Gardens. His mother moved her family to Baden; walking distance from Bellefontaine Neighbors and Riverview Gardens.

Jimmy decided early in life that he wanted to be a criminal. As he tells it, his dad worked for the MKT Railroad, and drowned while working during a flood in 1944. Jimmie rebelled after that incident.

 He started his career as a burglar. The region was awash with burglars, and it seemed like a simple way to make money. Break in when no one is at home and plunder anything you could find. Jimmy broke into Paul Cusamano's house on North Broadway and stole $500. Paul owned a produce stand on North Broadway, a cash and carry business, and had the cash on hand for Jimmy to Steal.

Jimmy blew the $500 immediately, drew attention to himself, and was arrested. He was sent to the Bellefontaine Reformatory on the bluffs of the Mississippi River. He escaped three times. Each time he hid in the Calvary Cemetery. Calvary and Bellefontaine (connected parcels) were the focal points of north St. Louis. It was and is almost like the citizens of the community can't wait to get there, permanently.

There are huge crypts for those who can afford them, and they make a great place to hide. Jimmy, obviously, got caught and taken back to the reformatory. He graduated from the eighth grade in reform school. He was sent to the city workhouse twice, and eventually The State Penitentiary in Jefferson City. It was said Jimmy burglarized the crypts in Calvary and Bellefontaine Cemeteries. He swears he didn't, and he swore he would never steal from the dead. Jimmy's got scruples!

Jimmy's older brother was an armed robber while Jimmy was burglarizing businesses and homes. The local sixth district cops called them Big Jelly Roll and Little Jelly Roll. The local cops knew them well. Big Jelly Roll was incarcerated in the Missouri State Penitentiary. Little Jelly Roll (Jimmy) robbed the Bettendorf Grocery Store on the Halls Ferry Circle when he was nineteen years old.

He scored $3000.00; he blew the cash extravagantly, was arrested and sent to the Missouri State Penitentiary. He and his brother Big Jelly Roll were brother/pal's in the joint. Jimmy exceled in incarceration. He got along with the other inmates and with the guards, even though his mantra in life was to hate authority.

Jimmy knew that if he was going to be a professional criminal, he needed a good criminal lawyer. Jimmy's mom approached Norm London, gave Norm $10,000 and hired him as Jimmy's lawyer. Norm London was loved by his clients. Jimmy, to this day still worships Norm London. He goes to Norm's grave every year on Norm's birthday. Norm London is a God to Jimmy.

But the strange thing about a guy like Norm London; he loved his clients, most of them, that is. The cop/writer had come into contact with and arrested big-time criminals who bragged about being personal friends with Norm London. It was laughed off; why would a low-life drug dealer, or robber, or any professional criminal be friendly with a smooth, educated guy like Norm London? His brother was the surgeon for the St. Louis Cardinals; they were educated, professional, classy, St. Louis royalty. Norm was the attorney for the St. Louis Metropolitan Police Department Union.

But it was true; Norm would allow dirtbag criminals, dope smugglers, the lowest of the low to hang around his law offices. He socialized with them. He invested hundreds of thousands of dollars in some of their drug smuggling schemes. At times, he worked for them pro bono. Jimmy Cochran was one of many.

Jimmy did approximately four years in Jefferson City for the Bettendorf's robbery. He got out and headed back to Baden. He worked as a laborer for a while, had a nice apartment, wore nice clothing, and had girlfriends. He was a man about town in Baden.

But, again, something snapped in Jimmy. He committed another armed robbery of a bank. A $1400 boondoggle, and was soon captured. He was on his way back to prison, this time he was sentenced to seventeen years in Leavenworth Federal Penitentiary. He received his high school equivalency diploma while in Leavenworth.

But when it came time for Jimmy to be set free from Leavenworth, the State of Missouri had him pinned for a liquor store robbery in St. Louis. A robbery Jimmy said he did not do. He was sent back to Jefferson City and

incarcerated for another ten years. All toll, Jimmy was
sent to the Missouri State Penitentiary three times, and
Leavenworth twice. Most criminals are not smart. Jimmy
proved this adage.

5

The city demographics continued to change, fueled by the fed. The north siders, German and Irish, were frantic; their once perfect world shattered by the changes. It became dangerous for them to leave their houses without being confronted by an irate and obviously hateful black person.

 Mundane chores like getting the mail from the mailbox, taking out the trash cans, became dangerous. Baden changed quickly. It is almost now 100% black. The busy retail area along North Broadway is abandoned. All of these demographic changes in the Federal town of St. Louis were done for two reasons: keep poor blacks reliant on the federal subsistence and keep them voting the Democrat ticket. It's why the population here, white and black, are so ignorant.

Businesses along Riverview Boulevard began to close. There was nowhere to shop for groceries; the Bettendorf Grocery Store (the one Jimmy Cochran robbed) was sold several times to local grocery chains and eventually closed. The Steak and Shake on the Halls Ferry Circle closed, and the Katz Drug store on Riverview Boulevard mysteriously burned. Most white folk headed north to Spanish Lake, and Florissant.

The town of Florissant was north west of Spanish Lake by several miles. It was predominantly white, and the German Catholic inhabitants wanted to keep it that way. The realtors in the area colluded to only allow conventional loans as the mortgage option.

Conventional loans required a twenty percent down payment. This kept this cop/writer from buying in

Florissant. They wouldn't accept the GI Bill option made available to vets. The collusion didn't pay off for them. Florissant is predominantly black at this time.

The burg of Jennings, connected to the City of St. Louis to the west was a bustling area for shopping. Restaurants, and almost anything a shopper would want was there for the purchase. The homeowners in Spanish Lake were certain they were safe from the push by the fed to make neighborhoods integrated.

Like the north city folk, they were certain there was no place for the fed to build housing projects. The fed didn't build; they made the luxury apartments section eight. They were subsidized for welfare blacks. The whites who had enjoyed the country club lifestyle of swimming pools and tennis courts were scrambling to get out of Spanish Lake.

The luxurious neighborhoods, like Fontaine Estates, with their vast lawns and large ranch style homes were also purchased using the infamous 235 loan. It changed neighborhoods overnight. The blacks moved in at night. People would wake up to find their neighbors were black, angry and hateful toward them. White flight was the only option.

But there was a resurgence in the Central West End (CWE). People of means were desiring to live in the giant art treasures on Hortense Place, Lennox Place, Pershing Place and Maryland that had been lying vacant for several years.

A developer, Leon Strauss, was purchasing properties and rehabbing them. Most of the grand old houses had been stripped of their fireplace mantels and decorative fireplace architecture. Some had grand fireplaces in almost every room, including the massive second and third floor bedrooms.

Many of the huge carved doors were also stripped from the homes, as well as stairway bannisters, and ornate glass light and sconces. These stolen items were fenced in and around the CWE at second hand or antique shops. At the time, no one cared. The grand old homes were probably going to be torn down, so what difference did it make?

But it made a difference to the new buyers of these gorgeous old homes. Many of the fireplace mantels had been sold to out of state buyers. People in California and in the eastern states desired them. Their neighborhoods were stable; untouched by phony oil crisis political moves from Washington D.C.; these folks were not at the mercy of the liberal politicians who scramble and plunder to get votes from minorities. The artwork from St. Louis now adorned their homes. St. Louis developers, rehabbers, and buyers had to start all over again.

The movers and shakers in St. Louis (people with cash) knew that the only way to bigger and better wealth was through the buying and selling of real estate. The CWE was the crown jewel of real estate in the region. Anchored by the Chase Park Plaza, the hotel where the rich and powerful stayed while in the region, and where future, past, and present presidents stayed, was owned by the Harold Koplar family.

They also owned a large portion of Maryland Plaza, a trendy dining and retail street with massive ornate homes on the north side, and lavish boutiques on the south side. The Mayor of the City of St. Louis, Alfonso Cervantes, also had real estate holdings along Maryland Plaza, and he was clamoring to own more.

Barnes and Jewish hospitals, two separate entities, were eventually going to merge, which meant the real estate along Forest park Boulevard from Kingshighway to Grand Avenue, east was going to be stabilized. The two hospitals combined would take up about a square mile of CWE space.

Forest Park, the other jewel of the city, was west of the CWE. St. Louis University was at Grand and Laclede, one block north of Forest Park Boulevard. The problem was the neighborhood connected to the CWE via Euclid Avenue north of Delmar; it was black ghetto then, and still is today.

Children of wealthy St. Louis families were taking real estate chances on Euclid Avenue, near McPherson. A vacant storefront at 405 N. Euclid was purchased and opened as a trendy, barebones night spot. The owner called it Timothy's. He was a young guy, maybe in his early twenties, and the place was getting traffic in the evening. He eventually sold the building and business to a guy named Herbie Carp from Chicago. Mr. Carp rebuilt it and opened an eclectic restaurant named Balaban's. The restaurant survived for decades and just recently closed.

At about the same time period (mid 70s) Llewellyn's Pub opened just east of Euclid on McPherson. A Pasta House Restaurant opened on the north east corner of Euclid and McPherson, and antique shops adorned both sides of McPherson in the 4700 block. The area was starting to come back to life.

With the Cervantes, Koplar, and Strauss families (as well as young entrepreneurs from wealthy families) sinking money into the CWE, police presence was demanded and granted. A beat cop was placed on Euclid and was expected to walk from Delmar (north) to Forest park Boulevard (south).

That was a lot of territory for one beat cop. So, a grant from the fed was requested and granted, and in the night hours, two beat cops walked Euclid and were paid an hourly wage. The beat went on in the CWE and it regained its luster. But the street crime was still there. People were being slain in the streets. Shoppers were being accosted coming and going.

The CWE, especially trendy Euclid Avenue, was a hunting ground for the blacks who lived north of Delmar. They could walk out of their houses, walk south on Euclid and punch, or steal or rob, and then run back across Delmar to the safety of their ghetto lifestyle.

It wasn't wrong in their minds for them to do this. They felt entitled to beat, steal and rob the rich, even though most of the customers coming and going to establishments were just working stiffs looking for a good time out with a girlfriend.

But the area held its own for decades. A lot of entrepreneurs made gobs of money on Euclid. The restaurant business is fickle. One quarter is good, two quarters bad, when the bad overcomes the good, the owners go out of business. When they did, on Euclid, there was always someone who thought they could do it better, and they rent the space and open their establishment. A lot of real good eating establishments came and went on Euclid. Black crime ended all of them. The owners of the buildings, the ones who purchased, them at a rock bottom price, kept getting richer.

The district cops, uniformed and working what the department called a "recreation schedule", a work schedule that showed every day off and every day worked for the entire year, were showing stress associated with combat.

The job description was, "answer the radio, complete your assignment, keep the peace, go to the next assignment, restore peace, go to the next assignment." Realistically, the job description was "answer the radio, go to address, fight with one or more black residents living at government subsidized home. Arrest person you fought with. Go to station with prisoner. Attempt to formally book him/her for charge of peace disturbance; fight him/her again, get help from any cop in the station, subdue prisoner. Take him/her to hospital. Return to district station and attempt to book again." This barrage of violence was never ending; cops were shooting people at will.

The district cops do most of the labor in the police department; it is top heavy with brass; people with family ties, political friends, and some cops who are just damned smart. But in most cases, for promoted cops, there's a politician in the closet. It didn't take much for a district cop to unload on some entitlement recipient.

We, district cops, were usually outgunned while answering calls or chasing street robbers and murderers. The police department issued .38 caliber revolvers. The ammunition they required that we carry was deficient. It wouldn't even go through a windshield of a car unless the shooter was right on top of the windshield. Cops were bringing deer rifles to work with them. Many of them were waiting for the big-day, when civil disobedience takes over and martial law is declared.

Crime and attitudes of police are cyclical; today's cops are waiting to be released upon the masses of protesting, burning, destroying criminals.

It seemed, to the untrained eye, that if and when a district cop shot someone, he was miraculously transferred to a downtown detective bureau, or at the very least, a district detective bureau, and given the title of "Detective."

It's what many of the district uniform cops desired. The uniform was a deterrent to their mental well-being. It had meaning inside and outside of the police department. It was blue collar; the bottom of the totem pole of life. It meant, in the eyes of other personnel, and casual observers outside of the police department, that you haven't tried hard enough; that you were lazy, second tier.

These observations were and are wrong. It was a mindset instilled by the hierarchy of the department to keep the working-class cops on edge. The desk jockeys of the police department were, and are, intelligent enough to know, that if the uniformed cops weren't doing their jobs, if for some strange reason they would stop answering calls, stop coming to work to be abused by the public, and their supervisors, they (the desk jockey brass) would be charged with going back to the streets and doing the work.

So, they smile and wink and spread false tales about promotions and transfers, and lazy cops, and bullheaded cops, and cops that don't wish to conform and the district cops acquiesce by shooting welfare blacks with big mouths, putting knives on their dead bodies, and injuring themselves so they can claim self-defense. It was, in those ancient days, all part of the program.

Another police department myth: if you killed someone in the line of duty you would be promoted and given a special job within the police department. Partially

true. Lieutenant Colonel John Doherty, Chief of
Detectives, was a killer of the "bad guy." He was famous
for it, like the old time Sheriff's and Marshall's of the old
west. His philosophy? Dead men don't talk.

In the City of St. Louis there was never a shortage of
"bad guys" to kill, and Chief John Doherty had
"shooters" within his Bureau of Investigation. The
requirement for being one of John Doherty's boys? Total
loyalty!

Even the Chicago Mafia, the crime syndicate who
took charge of all of or labor unions in the City of St.
Louis, and some of the trade unions, was in fear of John
Doherty and his group of cop detectives, but not enough
for them to return to Chicago. First, they had to plunder
the city's union coffers, and take care of their political
friends; state, local, and federal.

Department folklore, and cop gossip, run amok within
the halls of the old police headquarters building. There
were always rumors about John Doherty, killer,
schmoozer, hero. Cops wanted to be like him; no one
could. John Doherty had a sidekick, Detective Frank
Burns. He would do whatever John Doherty told him to
do. They were referred to as "specials" in the fifties,
when the Chicago Mafia came calling.

Doherty had a "special" black sedan, maybe an
Oldsmobile, and he kept it parked in the headquarters
garage. He got one for his sidekick, Frank Burns, also.
The windows were darkened with curtains, and
pedestrians were unable to see inside.

Folklore has it that when one of the Oldsmobile's was
gone from the garage, somebody was going to die. All of
the detectives in headquarters had their own personal take

home detective cars. The reasoning being, that we were on call twenty-four hours a day, and need a car at our disposal.

Frank Burns wrecked his in Chicago on a weekend jaunt. Nobody knew Frank was in Chicago, except maybe his mentor, John Doherty. There were a couple of questions the Internal Affairs Division wanted to ask Frank Burns, who by that time was a Detective Lieutenant in the prestigious Burglar-Robbery Division, Doherty's top killer squad.

One of the questions was: Why was Lieutenant Frank Burns, John Doherty's top killer, in Chicago? Internal Affairs Division, (IAD) was checking newspapers and conferring with the Chicago Police Department trying to determine if any organized crime czars had met their demise on this particular weekend. Frank was obviously on a secret mission for Detective Colonel John Doherty.

The other question was: If Frank Burns was on a holiday, why did he drive the police department car to Chicago? It is supposed to be used locally, for work related duties. IAD was prepared to grill Lieutenant Frank Burns. Doherty stepped into the fray: "I told him to use the department car. He was dispatched on a department assignment by me." End of story for the grilling of Lieutenant Frank Burns.

Lieutenant Frank Burns was a supervisor in the Bureau of Investigation. Burglary-Robbery was pure prestige. Anything a detective did in that unit was considered glamorous and above and beyond the call of duty.

Lieutenant Frank Burns had a brother who was associated with the Chicago Mafia, (The Outfit) and was deeply associated with the old Buster Wortman gang in

East St. Louis. Bobby Burns (Frank's brother) was a gangster.

It was common knowledge within the police department. Detectives from Intelligence (my unit) would pick him up on surveillance, meeting with the heads of the local unions, which meant the heads of the local Mafia branch. Bobby Burns, gangster, was a gun for hire. Killing must run in the family; the only difference between him and his brother Lieutenant Frank Burns was, Frank carried a badge and was protected by Detective Colonel John Doherty.

.

Captain John Doherty (his rank in the fifties) and Lieutenant Frank Burns were detectives in the Bureau of Investigation; killing the bad-guy was accepted, and expected. They had killed their share of street criminals.

Doherty had rank and power, even back in 1959. Frank Burns was a detective working for Doherty. The two of them talked about an upcoming robbery/murder of the owner of Star Vending in South St. Louis. Bobby Burns (Frank Burns' brother) and Marvin Dale Berry were supposed to rob and murder the Star Vending guy for a Chicago gangster, a local, and one of the upcoming Chicago style Mafia crooks in St. Louis.

The door to Doherty's office was open; all ears were on the conversation. "I'll kill him if you want me to," Frank Burns said to Doherty, referring to his brother, Bobby Burns. Doherty's response was muffled and unintelligible, but the message was there for all to hear, Frank Burns was willing to kill his own brother for John Doherty.

"Talk to your stupid brother and stop this idiotic plan from happening," John Doherty began.

Doherty drew on his cigar and blew a plume toward the ceiling. "No," Doherty again replied as if he was speaking to a pet. "Just stop cause for further complaint." Frank walked out of the office, took the elevator down to the lobby, walked to the parking lot and entered his detective car.

This communication between John Doherty and Frank Burns, was an example of the undying loyalty his followers had for him. There was nothing they would not do for John Doherty, even kill one's own brother.

The robbery of the vending machine owner happened. He had gotten word that the St. Louis Mafia wanted his business and were going to send an enforcer to intimidate, or kill him; he was waiting for Bobby Burns and Marvin Dale Berry to stroll in and act like tough guys. Bobby Burns was shot, wounded in the arm by the owner, captured and housed in the St. Louis City Jail. Marvin Dale Berry escaped but was eventually captured.

The Italian Mafia genius, (word on the street it was Tony Giordano) devised a plan to break Bobby Burns out of the city jail. At the time, the city jail was situated in downtown St. Louis, near the headquarters police station, west of city hall, and the city and state courts building. Also, alongside of the city jail was the children's Juvenile Detention Center, AKA the Children's Building.

Detective Robert Scheetz, received information that there was going to be an attempt to break Bobby Burns out of the city jail; Scheetz relayed his information to John Doherty. Bob Scheetz' information was that a guy named David Eugene Richardson, a career criminal and convicted rapist, and burglar, was to go to the children's side of the city jail.

An inmate (one who delivers prescription drugs to the other inmates) was ordered by Tony Giordano, or one of his lackeys to drop a line down from one of the upper windows of the city jail. David Eugene Richardson was supposed to tie a revolver to the string, and the guy on the other end was expected to draw the revolver up and into the window. The gun was to be given to Bobby Burns.

On March 18, 1959, Detective Robert Scheetz, Detective Al Tucci, and Lieutenant Frank Burns positioned themselves inside of the Juvenile Detention Center (Children's Jail) and waited. They had a clear shot at anyone who was walking around the north jail area.

David Eugene Richardson showed up; the cord was dropped from the window and Richardson was in the process of attaching the revolver to the string; Frank

Burns allegedly fired a warning shot from a twelve-gauge riot shotgun; Richardson allegedly tried to run and Frank Burns shot him with the riot gun and killed David Eugene Richardson. Bobby Burns was subsequently tried for the robbery of the vending machine owner; he got seventy-five years in the Missouri State Penitentiary.

Detective Robert Scheetz, the insanely intense Baden refugee, rose through the ranks and was eventually the Chief of Police for the City of St. Louis. Al Tucci's son, Kim Tucci, went into the restaurant business (Pasta House) with some friends and became successful. John Doherty was promoted to Lieutenant Colonel, and became the Chief of Detectives. Lieutenant Frank Burns continued as John Doherty's righthand killer.

David Eugene Richardson's death certificate states the cause of death was, hemorrhaging from multiple gunshots to the chest and abdomen. He would have had his Back turned to the detectives hiding in the Children's Building.

Maybe he turned when Frank Burns fired the warning shot; maybe someone (one of the detectives) shouted to him as he was attaching the pistol to the cord, he turned, and then was shot by Frank Burns. Had he run from the jail the wounds would have been in his back. Chief of Detectives, James E. Chapman, commended Lieutenant Frank Burns; he stated that if the pistol had gotten into the hands of Bobby Burns, it would have been disastrous. Frank Burns was a hero.

Detective Neil Kurlander, Burglary-Robbery, promoted to Lieutenant in the St. Louis Metropolitan Police Department, retired and became the Chief of Police in Maryland Heights, Missouri, worked for Lieutenant Frank Burns.

Detective Neil advised that Frank Burns was crazy, but cunning. He did not supervise any of the detectives in the unit. He was a supervisor by title only. Neil states that Frank Burns would make the detectives keep their own files concerning cases worked, and individual targets of investigation. He hardly spoke to any of the detectives under his tutelage.

Neil advised, that Lieutenant Frank Burns would drink Robitussin Cough Syrup with codeine which he kept in his drawer. He would gulp it, and then unload his pistol, and admire it. His fourth-floor desk window faced north with a view of City Hall (and the one-time location of the city jail and the Juvenile Detention Center).

Frank would gulp Robitussin, and then "dry fire" his pistol at people coming and going from City Hall. Dry fire is when someone aims and pulls the trigger of an unloaded weapon. That would be the extent of Lieutenant Frank Burns' day, except going to lunch with John

Doherty. Detective Neil figured Lieutenant Frank Burns had something on Colonel John Doherty, and that was the reason he was in the prestigious Burglary-Robbery Unit. "It certainly wasn't for his leadership skills," Neil stated.

6

Another police department myth was, "if you are already in a specialized unit, and you kill a bad guy, you would be revered and promoted to sergeant." Many of the cops in the department believed this perverted tale as the gospel. The myth was ludicrous and dangerous. It made already over stressed and desperate cops, murderous monsters.

Most cops desired to be promoted. Some wanted to be a detective in the Intelligence Unit. We sometimes get what we desire, and if the cop's luck holds, he/she will have a good riding partner, like Detective Tom Rangel. Tom was, and is a smart guy, and he was meticulous about documenting the many crooks we came into contact with in a day's work.

Our job description was to investigate organized criminals and organized crime groups. That equated to the Chicago Mafia who infiltrated our town and took control of most of the union and trade unions. But there were times when the union crooks couldn't be found, or when out of boredom, we would look for street crime to brighten our day.

The big-deal of most days was, toward the end of our shift, to cruise the bloody ninth district, spot a black guy in a car who we figured was carrying a gun, and to stop and frisk him, and arrest him for Carrying A Concealed Weapon.

Of course, the gun was seized and carried to the department laboratory and test fired. The bullet was then compared to every bullet taken from a dead corpse (unsolved murder victim) in the past fifty years. Several homicides a year were solved by this unlawful search and seizure.

But the cop got recognition; our boss was satisfied that we were trying to be hot-shot detectives, and that we weren't wasting our time. In reality, this method of unlawful search and seizure was a way to seize firearms from ghetto residents.

 It was gun confiscation at its finest. It is now legal for anyone, twenty-one, with a non-felony record, in the State of Missouri to conceal carry. It was archaic law enforcement, and against the second amendment of the constitution. But it was done for decades in the City of St. Louis. The guns were eventually melted down and made into manhole covers.

Thousands of guns a year were seized, tested, and destroyed. Did these seizures make a difference in the crime statistics? Doubtful! St. Louis has always ranked toward the top of murders; murder city, that's our slogan.

There was a new crime tactic becoming prevalent in the St. Louis area, especially in the black neighborhoods: carjacking. These crime trends begin, and the street cop never knows how they are adopted so easily by the black subculture in America, but they are.

Two bozos, Darryl Sadler, and Jerry Bell, decided to carjack a sixty-three-year-old woman, who was fortunate enough to own a Cadillac sedan. Darryl Sadler decided he should rape her, as well as steal her car, so the two abducted the old gal, Darryl did his thing with her, then they ejected her from her Caddy, and drove off. Darryl advised her she could get her car at Grand and Cass.

The victim called the police and advised the officers that she was told they were going to leave her Caddy at Grand and Cass. It didn't take a genius to figure out where to spend the next couple of hours. They pulled up and we blocked the intersection with our undercover cop car. Darryl pointed a gun at us and we started firing at the two of them with our little .38 five shot pistols.

Tom had mentioned during our travels, that he wished he would get a chance to kill a bad guy so he could get promoted. Being a sergeant was a big deal to him; he was obsessed with it.

We fired several rounds into the windshield of the Caddy, while Darryl Sadler was backing up on North Grand at a high rate of speed. He backed quickly into a service station, threw it in drive and drove north on North Grand. With one round of ammo left in the detective .38, the rear window of the Caddy was blown out. Cops converged on the Caddy about three blocks away, and the two bad guys were arrested.

As this tumultuous event ended, and we regained our composure, if there is such a thing, being a cop detective in the City of St. Louis, we decided to grab a couple of beers after work and talk things over. It took two days for us to get our heads straight and we had been silent about the event, which is not healthy.

After a couple of cold ones, Tom opened up. "We should have killed those dirty rapist bastards."

"We tried, we did everything we could, it just didn't work in our favor." That was actually a lie. Upon viewing the forensic photos of the Caddy, all of our shots were low, almost to the dashboard of the Caddy, not high where the heads of the rapists and carjackers were seated, pointing pistols at us.

"We would have been promoted," Tom mumbled.

Some research on this killing/promoted myth was much needed. "There's a bunch of cops who kill a lot of bad guys and don't get promoted, who's that cop out in the seventh district? He's shot a bunch of guys, killed a bunch, too, do you remember his name?"

"Glen Stovall," Tom replied. "He's a shooter on and off duty."

"Yeah, and he's still in the seventh, in uniform." (Glenn Stovall shot eleven people in a twenty-four-year span, five of them died from their wounds.)

"But he's not in a specialized unit," Tom replied. "We are, and we are under a microscope at all times. Everybody's watching us. Had we killed one or both of those pieces of filth, we would have gotten on the promotion list."

I thought about Glenn Stovall; he was a slow talking country sounding cop, quick with a grin and a nice guy to talk to. He was visiting his brother in Madison County, Illinois, his brother owned a service station/garage. Two guys came in a started fighting with the Glenn's brother, so Glenn shot them both.

The liberal/socialist St. Louis newspaper reported that Glen had been indicted for the shootings in Edwardsville, which would have been easy to believe; Madison County, Illinois is a cesspool of jurisprudence, but it was fake news by a fake newspaper. They wrote a retraction.

Glen also shot a couple of guys while working secondary for Laclede Gas. The security company who had the contract with Laclede Gas, Whelan Security, was sued by a relative of one of the guys Glen shot. Glen testified on the stand, professionally, and was questioned about the people he had shot in his career. Internal Affairs had investigated all of Glen Stovall's shooting incidents and had determined he was within his professional duty to shoot.

The law in Missouri at that time stated that a peace officer could shoot a fleeing felon. It was revised that the felon should be a danger to the public, or a police officer, but that was not a problem in the City of St. Louis, Missouri.

Tom Rangel was correct in one aspect of his theory; Glen Stovall was taken off of the streets and placed in an office job in headquarters, weekends off. Promotion? Maybe. Stuck in an office for eight hours a day: not a street cop's style.

It took some brain racking to counter Tom's shooting theory. If you live by the sword...... going out onto the street every working day with Tom and have to be concerned about him shooting someone, just for the possibility of being miraculously promoted to sergeant was alien in theory and practice.

Although, almost all of the promotions were miraculous. To the cops being promoted, it was akin to immaculate conception. To working street cops, the promotional process was disgusting; an event invented to make desperate cops overreact on trivial violations of the law so they can be noticed by a few ego freak supervisors with politicians in their closets.

At night when we would ply the bloody ninth district looking for gangsters, or street criminals, driving in the little detective staff car, Tom had his .38 snub pistol in his hand. He was prepared to shoot first, ask questions later.

Detective Greg Chase came to mind as fodder for a good argument against "shoot first and ask questions later." "Greg Chase, in the vice unit; he's shot a bunch of guys, killed a couple, and he's never been promoted. And an old guy in the bloody ninth district, Bert Milberg. He's shot several guys; never promoted or moved into a specialized unit. Bill Hawkins, shot a bunch of guys, killed some; never promoted. And Roy Forester, old ninth district guy. He shot and killed a guy behind the ninth district station; never promoted." (although years later, Roy married a female who was friendly with Ron "Bubba" Henderson, the new black chief of police, and he was miraculously promoted). He was forced to retire because he couldn't pass the physical fitness test. To the casual observer, it seemed those were the types of people who were promoted. Tom didn't seem to mind being lumped together with them.

The bottom line was: most City of St. Louis cops mimicked Detective Colonel John Doherty. They worshipped him. He shot criminals. He was a friend to wealthy businessmen. He belonged to an exclusive country club and played golf with the upper echelon of St. Louis society. He was feared and admired by all who met him.

But John Doherty was still a "cop". A St. Louis cop; a place where cops are underpaid, looked down upon, and must hustle to survive. John Doherty hustled; he had two jobs, had children who never saw him. He wasn't, nor is any St. Louis cop, the kind of guy who comes home from work to dinner, exchanges ideas with his family, gives guidance, nurtures, leads, directs his family through their daily routines, goes to bed early so he can get up fresh and head to the office.

That isn't the life of a St. Louis cop. The job consumes all family time. The second job separates the head of the family from most family gatherings. The only thing nurtured is the cop's image and reputation. He's like a film star; always on stage, always recognized, stared at, revered, but hated by some and worshipped by others. This is the life some cops strive for. They will do anything to achieve "cop stardom." Lie, cheat, steal, kill.

On the evening of December 14, 1982, Donna and Gary Decker were walking to their car in the Grandpa Pigeons parking lot in Bellefontaine Neighbors, Missouri. It is situated in north St. Louis County, and had been targeted for drastic demographic change with the influx of thousands of welfare blacks, guided by the federal government's plan to make everything north in the St. Louis region, black.

Donna Decker was Detective Tom Rangel's sister, Gary was his brother-in-law. They were young and vibrant with two young children, and they had been Christmas shopping for friends and family. When they got to their car, they were approached by two black guys, armed with a handgun.

The two men: Raphael Clark, and Walter Harvey, demanded money from the Decker's, and then decided they were also going to abduct Donna Decker. Her husband tried to protect his wife, and he was shot in the chest. The bullet ripped into Gay Decker's heart, killing him instantly.

The two assailants placed Gary Decker's body into the back seat and leaned it so it was in a sitting position. Donna Decker was placed in the front seat. They drove to East St. Louis, Illinois, drove onto railroad property, shot Donna Decker in the head, four times, and left both bodies there.

The investigation was huge. Tom was in shock, and every detective in the Intelligence Unit felt his pain. It was a terrorist attack on anyone white living in north St. Louis or north St. Louis County. This was a blue-collar-working-class-community; people who lived here were trapped by their lower middle-class poverty. They worked to pay off their homes, had meager savings, and now had nowhere to go. The tidy streets their homes sat on were now warzones.

There were witnesses to the abduction and shooting of Gary Decker. A witness observed the terrorist abductors with Donna Decker in the front seat and Gary Decker in the back seat. The driver, Raphael Clark grinned at the witness, showing his gold tooth. The Decker car continued on and took the Poplar Street Bridge to Illinois.

The case stalled for a while, but eventually, Raphael Clark and Walter Harvey bragged about the murders to some of their friends. Clark stated that he shot Gary Decker because Gary was trying to be a hero.

Most of our Intelligence Unit coworkers lived in north St. Louis County. People who could, moved south, but cops were hampered by a residency rule stating they could not live outside of St. Louis County.

Tom moved south. Later in the cop/crook game, luck was with the cop/writer with a move south to Oakville. Targeted neighborhoods changed the face of the entire St. Louis region.

Tom was never the same after the murders of his sister and brother-in-law. There's always irony in the cop job. It was ironic that our two-man team arrested black terrorists on a daily basis. Occasionally we would arrest a white hoodlum, but our endeavors were mostly fueled by black criminals. But we didn't kill any of them. We arrested hundreds of big-time criminals and only had gun-play onetime.

We discussed this glaring fact; we always had the advantage; we were aggressive and in control. Terrorist

criminals are looking for easy targets. The easier a
potential victim is, the worse they are treated. Donna
Decker was heard by a witness pleading for Raphael
Clark and Walter Harvey not to hurt her. They fed on her
fear of them; murdered Gary, the love of her life, and her
protector, before her very eyes.

Nobody knows what life has in store for them. For the
cop, it's retirement; it's what we strive for. We make up
images of our lives once we are retired; beaches, cars and
maybe even a boat. Unless you inherit gobs of cash, this
is only a pipe dream fueled by the thoughts of the cops
dying around you; the ones who smoked and drank and
hardly slept, caught up in the race to, wherever.

It wasn't for Tom. He retired at twenty years. That
meant he got forty percent of his base pay for the rest of
his life. No dreams coming to life there. His wife had,
and has a good paying job, so he isn't destitute. The
terroristic murder of his sister devastated him and he
never recovered.

7

Back to the Bloody Ninth District: The cop/writer had a new riding partner, Glen Vaughn. He was an old-time cop, which meant he had maybe, ten years, on the department. Anything over ten years was unusual, unless it was a supervisor. So many cops came into the cop job thinking they were going to become stars overnight; they get disillusioned quickly and leave after a few years.

Glen Vaughn was a hard charger. Some cops hire on to be supervisors. Some just want to lock up the bad-guy. Kind of like Dirty Harry Callahan, and so many other movie and television cop heroes. Glen was one of those, and maybe we all are at the beginning.

Glen had been assigned to the Narcotics/Vice Unit. A specialized unit; all of us young/new cops, wished to be in such a unit. To us, it was true police work. Free of the uniform, the radio, the supervisors always breathing down your neck. He mesmerized us with his stories of being an undercover detective in a dangerous and rotten town like St. Louis. Narcotics investigation was crude and unchartered territory.

Glen was different from any other cop we young cops had come into contact with. He'd been indoctrinated to seek out and to arrest real bad-guys. He'd been in the trenches, inside of the crime scene tape to places only hardened criminals and undercover cops dare tread.

The murder of Detective Mel Wilmoth had burned a hole in Glen's brain. Glen was there that horrid night when a group of detectives wanted to gain entry to an apartment at 6152 Waterman. Dope was being used and sold there. The detectives were in the stinking hallway, (these old wooden buildings stink from years of filth. The wood is permeated and the stench never leaves the mind of visiting cops), drinking beer and listening to the activity inside of the apartment.

They were whispering to one another, trying to get a game plan down so someone would open the door and they could burst in, arrest everyone, and seize drugs.

Search warrants were something new to law enforcement in cities like St. Louis. There had to be an affidavit, an informant who was reliable, and had showed his or her reliability several times in the past. A state judge had to sign off and issue the warrant.

Cops and federal agents casually lie in search warrant affidavits. The informant does not have to be identified. He is protected by the legal process. Most informants are made up by the cop's, or agent's supervisor. In the cop/crook business, nothing beats success. Lying makes search warrant affidavits legal documents; a state or federal judge, or magistrate, believes the information in the affidavit; he gives the warrant to break in, search and seize contraband.

It happened in the Donald J. Trump presidential campaign; The FBI drew up a phony F.I.S.A. (Foreign Intelligence Surveillance Act) affidavit with bogus information about a ghost informant. It worked for the FBI. It works for city cops. But Glen Vaughn and his band of merry narcs didn't have a warrant.

In the minds of the detectives, if the door was opened by someone inside of the apartment, they would not need a search warrant. So, someone got the idea to kick a beer can up and down the hallway, causing a ruckus, so that someone inside would open the door, and they could rush in.

They did it; the door opened, and they rushed in. A paranoid, drug-high, transient from California shot the first person he saw coming through the doorway. It was Detective Mel Wilmoth. Several detectives opened fire on the apartment shooter, killing him. Glen was one of them.

Neil Kurlander, (previously mentioned in this nonfiction book) retired Chief of Police for Maryland Heights, Missouri, was a member of the Bureau of Investigation with Detective Mel Wilmoth. The bureau was rotating detectives in and out of the Narcotics Division. It was Neil Kurlander's turn to go to the Narcotics Division to work for a year or so. Neil didn't want to go, but Neil's the kind of guy who plays the cards as they are dealt to him. He was preparing for the exchange.

An old cop advised Neil when he was a rookie, not to take a job in narcotics; there's a bad stigma with narcotics work, and the general public, and other high-ranking cops (who are honest) in the department feel the narcotics cop is tainted and crooked.

Detective Mel Wilmoth volunteered to go in the place of Neil Kurlander. Neil gladly accepted Mel's offer. Mel was a killer/shooter. He had killed two guys already in his brief career; one was questionable, an unarmed burglar in a parking lot building. Mel was a hotshot, carried a nickel- plated six-inch magnum revolver, and he was a big talker. One of his sayings was, "When I die, I want to be cremated, my ashes placed in a douche bag and run through one more time."

Neil stood by Mel Wilmoth's coffin during the funeral as part of the honor guard, dress uniform, white gloves and a stone face. It was Neil's responsibility to remove

Mel's badge from his dress uniform as he lay in the coffin. Mel was twenty-eight years of age; he had seven years on the police department.

Skip Rudiger was the famous narcotics/cop detective of that particular time frame, and personally assigned to narcotics. Neil was friends with him; they drank together, partied together and went boating together.

The drug raids were always unlawful; kick in the door without a warrant and arrest. When questioned about the raids, the narcotics guys would say they were from another unit within the Bureau of Investigation. Everyone was working drugs in one form or another. Snitches were always trying to help themselves on a charge by snitching on druggies.

There wasn't much control within the bureau; cops did what they wanted to do; that was the call of the wild back in the day. If you screwed up, you went back to uniform, dried out, and possibly saved your marriage, and your life.

As was usually the case, the unit was broken up. Detectives were stripped of their ceremonious title and sent back to uniform. Glen got saddled with the cop/writer. That's the law of the land in a cop car, riding shoulder to shoulder, and depending on each other if and when things get rough.

The cop dissects his partner, like a psychologist, or a relative. If thoughts were bullet's they would be zipping around inside the patrol car as the cops go from to call to call, threatening, calming, correcting, and arresting.

The death of Mel Wilmoth deeply touched every detective on the scene, but Glen was silent and contemplating; within himself and scary. Every move he

made in the car was noted by his riding partner. But his
cop detective stories were fun to listen to.

Jimmy Kitterman was another highly decorated cop
from the Bureau of Investigation who came to the ninth
district, stripped of his ceremonious title, Detective. Most
of the young cops rode with him occasionally; we got
along, but Jimmy didn't talk about his Detective career;
he was angry, dangerous, and he gave people the
impression he would kill first and ask questions later.
Some cops didn't enjoy working with him.

Jimmy quit, and eventually was incarcerated for an
unknown offense. He got out and moved to Schiller Place
in south city. It was poor folk paradise, white ghetto. The
cop/writer was detached to DEA, the Task Force, and a
United States Attorney, Debbie Herzog (big friends with
city and county cops) had information that Jimmy
Kitterman was dealing cocaine. She wrote up a search
warrant affidavit, took a task force detective, and the
search warrant affidavit before a federal magistrate; the
detective swore that he had a confidential informant,
reliable three times in the past, and the magistrate issued
the warrant.

In the Task Force, we all participated in search
warrants; the cop/writer refused to go on the warrant.
Jimmy Kitterman was at one time a fellow cop, in a
police car, in the bloody ninth district. Reluctance led to
being excused.

The task force executed the warrant; there was a
condom stuffed with white powder, resembling cocaine.
Jimmy was not present at the time of the search warrant
execution. The condom was brought to the task force
offices; a field test was done on the condom ingredients;
the white powder was not a controlled substance.

As was always the case, DEA Task Force officers seized paperwork inside of the dwellings search warrants were executed on. Among Jimmy Kitterman's papers was a business card, crudely made from a copy machine, stating his name, Private Investigator, his phone number and, under his name was, "Ex-cop, Ex-con."

Unlike most stoic cops, Glen Vaughn was superstitious, and he believed in Karma. Our Watch Commander was Lieutenant Robert Scheetz. Glen didn't like him; Bob Scheetz was all police department, an intense company man; Bob Scheetz desired to be the Chief of Police, and he eventually made it.

Glen Vaughn wanted to be a detective in the St. Louis Metropolitan Police Department and lock up bad guys. He made it, and then it was taken from him. His career choices were not maintainable. He had painted himself into a corner with no escape route. Bob Scheetz had an escape plan; keep making rank.

Remember the movie, my reading friend, The French Connection? Gene Hackman and Roy Scheider, two New York City Narcotics Detectives were in a night spot and they spot something out of the ordinary, two people spending gobs of money that they did not have. They begin to wonder where these two paper delivery people, who they were familiar with, got the money to burn. Remember the eerie music accompanying the looks by Gene Hackman; the cop stare? The conspiracy burn? It actually happens that way. Narcotics detectives, and Intelligence Unit Detectives have been there. It burns a hole in your brain; it energizes you and you desire more information. It's like a fishing lure being dragged past a giant fish. The cops are the fish. The cop Detective wants to eat and assimilate the bait, and everything around it.

Glen Vaughn was going through cop investigator rehab. In the cop business, anyone can be a great detective. He just has to apply himself, ignore his wife, children, supervisors, and any moral value he has, and he or she is in business.

Nobody cares about the title, except the detective. Glen was going through conspiracy withdrawal, like a heroin addict sitting in solitary confinement, or an alcoholic dreaming of the first drink of the day. The conspiracy burn is gone forever for the exiled cop detective.

Glen knew it, but he refused to accept this fact. So, he told young uniformed cops, stories, and we drove around the bloody ninth district, trying to restore peace; another impossible task.

Those cop detective jobs aren't there for lifetime careers; they are there for the "recipient of the title, detective", to do his best, learn about career criminals, and then to get promoted and move on.

In the "cops and robbers" game, you either move up, move on, or move back. None of us desire to move back. That's no fun, so the detective over-extends himself by over doing, getting case after case, drinking in excess, thinking he is endearing himself to the bosses, who are just looking for the chance of getting promoted again.

It was not difficult to make a comparison to Glen Vaughn, and this cop didn't want to be like him, a washed-up old detective with a drinking problem, ruined by the system because he took the wrong path. But the system chooses, not the cop. The system chose him to be a cracker jack detective, burn out, and to come back to mediocrity seeking refuge, like a wounded animal.

It could happen to any of us young cops who don't worship the command rank. They were mostly frazzled robots, doing paperwork, using overkill to please their bosses in headquarters, chained to a desk like clerks with guns and badges.

The commanders in the police department soon learn what motivates certain cops. A position of status within; a take home car; a promotion. They use your weakness to make you work harder; threatening and plotting on how to harass the employee.

That lifestyle did not appeal to all cops. It is easy to imagine oneself as the confident detective, kind of a happy medium between Sherlock Holmes, and Detective Frank Bullitt.

So, the detective, Glen Vaughn, is back in a police car, wearing a uniform, jonesing for the thrill of the hunt and the capture, and if he still has a wife, or family to go home to, the wife is contemplating divorce, demands he stop drinking beer at home, and the kids don't like him. So, it was young cops and Glen Vaughn in a cop car in the bloody ninth district.

James Leroy Cochran, (Jimmy), was released from Leavenworth for his latest armed robbery. He went back to Baden and lived a quiet life, working and dressing well, living a good clean life. He had a nice apartment, dressed like a suave businessman, and he had a girlfriend. By all accounts, he had been rehabilitated; he even had a St. Louis cop friend, Patrolman Bill Monroe, and Bill Monroe's wife, Marilyn, whom he hobnobbed with.

Jimmy was dissatisfied with the boring lifestyle referred to as, survival. He desired, and he decided, that he was entitled to more than the average Joe on the street; he was, for all intents and purposes, a famous bank robber from Baden. Everyone knew his name; he carried celebrity status.

He asked a friend (a person he refuses to identify) to supply him with a car, preferably stolen, and a pistol. Jimmy still carries the invisible "oath of silence" used by inmates in jails like the Missouri State Penitentiary, and the federal prison, Leavenworth. Jimmy is still a criminal, in the same manner alcoholics and drug addicts are still addicted; they just have it under control.

Only straight Johns on the outside rely on the old saying, "There's no honor among thieves." In the incarceration business, snitches die. In Jimmy's mind, he could be back on the inside at any moment. He refuses to divulge any information on anyone else, just himself.

Jimmy had a plan to rob the Cass Federal Savings and Loan Association at 8308 North Broadway in Baden. Jimmy had been planning the robbery for months. He wanted revenge for the ten years he spent in the Missouri Penitentiary for a robbery he did not commit. He was angry, mad, and vengeful.

Paul Lockhart, a friend whom he met in Leavenworth, telephoned Jimmy. Paul was living in rural Leslie, Missouri. He couldn't find employment; his wife worked at a corncob pipe factory in Washington, Missouri. He was broke, and broken, and he asked Jimmy for help; he wanted to know if Jimmy knew of anyone who was planning a "job". He wanted in.

Jimmy trusted Paul Lockhart. Jimmy told Paul to come to his apartment in Baden, and they would discuss the job. Paul was there the next day. There were no elaborate plans; no masks, just tape on their faces, sunglasses and ball caps, no plans for escape, just go in, announce a robbery and take whatever was available. Jimmy was begging for death, or at the very least, another trip to Leavenworth. He actually liked it there. To him, the federal penitentiary was peaceful, quiet, and creative, and (he told me) the food was good.

The car he requested was parked at the rear of a department store on North Broadway. The pistol he asked for was in the glove box. There was a note: "Burn the car when you are through with it. Bring the pistol back to me." Jimmy had a bottle of gasoline with a wick attached to it. He learned about Molotov cocktails in Leavenworth. He carefully placed the bomb on the floor near the backseat.

The streets of Baden were a stage for Jimmy, and he was about to perform for his fanatics. Jimmy drove the blue Pontiac to the bank, parked illegally in front, and he and Paul Lockhart jumped out of the Pontiac and rushed into the bank.

They shouted at the customers to get against the wall and to not look at them. Jimmy had a white pillowcase and he stuffed it with cash. All in all, they had robbed the bank of $10,000, so they ran to the illegally parked Pontiac and took off.

A bank employee hit the bank alarm, and another employee jotted down the license number of the blue Pontiac getaway car. The police dispatcher broadcasted the description of the car, and the robbers, within minutes.

Jimmy drove the Pontiac to East Railroad Avenue and Hall Street and burned it with the Molotov cocktail.

There was another car waiting for them, a black Mercury. He and Paul Lockhart jumped in and drove toward North Broadway. Jimmy ran a red light at North Broadway and East Railroad. A cop on patrol observed them and attempted to pull them over. Jimmy wouldn't pull over and he drove toward Interstate 70. The cop, Patrolman Kenneth Becker, continued after them, trying to stop them before Jimmy could get onto the Interstate, but Jimmy jumped on the Interstate and headed west.

Patrolman Becker was not aware he was chasing a vehicle with two bungling criminals who had just robbed the Cass Federal Savings and Loan. He was just going to cite them for a traffic violation and make his supervisor a happy man.

As Patrolman Becker pursued, Lockhart leaned out of the car and fired six shots at the police car. They all missed; Jimmy was known for never harming anyone in his self-destructive robbery games. He just liked the excitement and the attention, and he didn't mind federal incarceration. Lockhart had a mean streak and he wanted to kill Patrolman Becker; he just wasn't a good shot.

Jimmy and Paul Lockhart continued west on I-70, with Patrolman Becker in pursuit. Lockhart reloaded and fired six more shots at the patrol car. Becker fired back striking the trunk of the Mercury. Lockhart reloaded again and fired six more times. Jimmy saw the Riverview Boulevard exit, and he took it.

There was a roadblock of cop cars; Jimmy told Lockhart to hang on, that he was going to ram the roadblock. Lockhart got down on the floor of the car and covered his head. At the last second, Jimmy saw the service station at Lillian and Riverview; he drove through the station lot, missing the pumps and cars, and came out the other side, sideways.

The Mercury crashed into a curb, both Jimmy and Lockhart were thrown from the Mercury. Jimmy managed to hold onto his revolver. He had two pockets full of ammunition; he was going to shoot it out with the sixth district cops. Paul Lockhart told Jimmy he was going to give himself up. Jimmy told him to lie flat on the ground, that if he got up on his feet, they would shoot and kill him. Paul spread out on the pavement as Jimmy sought cover behind the getaway car, crashed Mercury.

The cops shot hundreds of rounds of ammunition at Jimmy as he hid behind the Mercury. The Mercury took most of the shots. Jimmy was firing back, as Paul Lockhart laid on the street and waited to be handcuffed, or shot. Jimmy shot and reloaded, and the shots kept coming at him and the Mercury.

Jimmy saw his chance; he glanced over at Northwest High School and observed some students out on the football field. He ran for the school as shots were being fired at him, whizzing by his head and thumping into the ground around him, one of them struck him in the arm.

Greg Tuck was a student at Northwest High School at the time. He was in class, he knew Jimmy Cochran, and he mused about the incident as it was going down.

There was a door at the gym on the south side of the school; it was partially open. He ran for it. He saw someone attempting to close the door, Jimmy yelled at the person to leave the door open. The guy stopped and looked at Jimmy, who by that time had a gun pointed at the man.

There was mass confusion inside the school; the gun battle had disturbed the students and they were pouring out of the classrooms.

Don LaPlante, head football coach and administrative assistant, observed the gun battle from the second floor of the school; he ran down to lock the school doors to keep Jimmy out, and to keep the students from leaving the building. But it was too late; Jimmy was already inside.

LaPlante could do nothing but stare at Jimmy. Jimmy was standing in front of him with a pistol pointed at LaPlante's midsection. "You're going with me," Jimmy growled at the coach. With the gun at his back, LaPlante walked in front of Jimmy down the hallway. They were confronted by Patrolman Tony Beal. "Get out of the way or I'll kill him," Jimmy shouted. "Put your gun on the floor and slide it over to me with your foot."

Beal knew Jimmy Cochran, just like most cops in the Baden and Walnut Park neighborhoods. Tony smiled at Jimmy, shook his head in disbelief, and moved out of their way.

Tony Beal refused to give up his weapon. Most cops know that if you give up your gun, you're going to be beaten to death, or just shot in the face. Jimmy and LaPlante continued down the hallway until they reached the north door.

Jimmy left LaPlante behind and ran down Riverview Boulevard, pursued by Patrolman Tony Beal and a bevy of other sixth district cops. They couldn't catch him. Jimmy was home free on the streets he grew up on.

Jimmy was almost broke (the $10,000 was left behind in the Black Mercury). He entered a house just a few blocks away from Northwest High School through an unlocked back door. He waved his pistol at the couple inside and told them to keep quiet or he would kill them.

Jimmy calmed down and began talking to the couple. Their 10-month-old granddaughter and their 2-year-old grandson were in the house; eventually other relatives came home and there were fourteen people being held hostage by Jimmy Cochran.

Jimmy paced, danced, drank whiskey, and snacked on cheese, and eventually figured it was time for him to move on. He ordered the man of the house to get him the keys to his car, and to accompany him. He ordered the other family members to not call the police for fifteen minutes.

The two of them took off, the hostage driving and Jimmy in the backseat. Jimmy had the hostage stop at a convenience store in a shopping center (Grandpa Pigeons) where Jimmy purchased a box of .38 caliber bullets.

Jimmy asked the hostage how much money he had; the hostage replied, "$20.00." Jimmy told him to keep it, and eventually they ended up in Illinois near the I-270 and route #3 intersection. Jimmy set the hostage free. He called his family and they called the City cops, and he was picked up and questioned. He said Jimmy was nice to him.

The hostage freely talked about his encounter with the famous bank robber, James Leroy Cochran. He advised the police that Jimmy was wounded and bleeding heavily from a wound in his left arm and he was also wounded in his left leg, apparently from the gun fight outside of the high school.

On the evening of October 22nd, a frantic woman called police headquarters in St. Louis and advised she had been abducted by James Leroy Cochran at her home in Boonville, Missouri, about 150 miles west of St. Louis. He had followed her into her home while she was carrying in groceries and when she tried to flee, Jimmy threatened her with a pistol.

Jimmy told her she was coming with him. She advised him she needed to go to the bathroom. She attempted to use a lipstick to write a message on the mirror, but Jimmy walked in on her and erased the message. He slapped her when she again attempted to flee from him. They headed for Kansas City in the new hostage' Cadillac.

There was a newspaper; Jimmy showed her newspaper clippings of the bank robbery, and the shootout near Northwest High School. She advised that they drove around Kansas City for a while and then headed east toward St. Louis. Jimmy stopped the Cadillac in north St. Louis and told her to get out. She gladly exited the vehicle and Jimmy drove away in her car.

At 2200 hours that night Patrolmen Patrick Jones and Otto Hirsch observed a Cadillac matching the description of the vehicle taken in Boonville parked at the curb on Theobold Street in north St. Louis. The officers parked behind the vehicle and started to get out, intending to check the driver.

Suddenly the driver (Jimmy) dove out of the Caddy and fired three shots at the officers. One of the bullets struck the police car. Jimmy ran through an alley and eluded Patrolmen Jones and Hirsch. Otto Hirsch radioed for help and approximately 100 police officers flooded the area looking for Jimmy the bank robber.

A helicopter, which was probably borrowed from the Highway Patrol, aided in the search. It flew back and forth across the area beaming its powerful searchlight down on the ground. People were coming out of their houses and looking at the helicopter. They couldn't find Jimmy. Jimmy told me that when the helicopter shined the light near him, he stopped and froze.

As the search continued Jimmy was spotted on a railroad overpass on North Broadway near Calvary, more shots were exchanged. It seemed that Jimmy had lost his mind and turned violent. Jimmy was headed back to his old hiding place, Calvary Cemetery. He knew every crack and crevice in the graveyard and could burrow in and hide. A cop walked right by him and did not see him.

Jimmy hid and slept in and out of the rain that night while the cops walked by him and the helicopter flew over him. Jimmy crawled out of Calvary Cemetery and headed for north St. Louis County. He observed a man (John L. Dorrell III) in a parking lot and abducted him. He and Dorrell headed west and ended up in Albuquerque New Mexico.

Jimmy was trying to touch base with a Leavenworth Penitentiary convict friend, Arthur David Scott, (Scotty). Jimmy called the phone number he had gotten from Scotty. Scotty's parents answered; Jimmy told them who he was. They advised Jimmy that the FBI had already been there looking for him, and that he should stay away from their home. They told him Scotty was living in Ohio, and working for National Cash Register Company, (NCR.) Jimmy headed back toward St. Louis.

Cops and the FBI were speculating Jimmy would come back to Baden, release his hostage and head for Calvary Cemetery. It was also speculated Jimmy was suicidal and wanted to die in a spectacular shootout with cops in Calvary Cemetery.

Patrolman Glen Vaughn, cop partner, and this cop/writer, had been on recreation (days off). We both had heard of the manhunt for James Leroy Cochran. The cop/writer's residence was in the 8800 block of Riverview Boulevard. The police helicopter buzzed our tiny apartment all night long. It was easy to rationalize that Jimmy was a sixth district problem, not a cop assigned to the bloody ninth district.

It was the night watch for us, 11:00 p.m. to 7:00 a.m. Every watch is screwy in any big city, but it is extra screwy on the night watch in St. Louis, Missouri. We went to rollcall and after rollcall headed for a beat car. A sergeant assigned to the ninth from another district, Phil Pizzo, approached us. "You guys are on a detail tonight, check out two shotguns and meet me in the command office," he ordered.

We acquired two 12-gauge Remington pump shotguns from the desk officer and headed into the command office. "I guess you guys know about the manhunt in the sixth district, right? The hunt for James Leroy Cochran?"

"Yes, sir." Glen Vaughn did not speak; he briefly glared at the sergeant. His disdain for command rank officers was apparent in everything he did. Sergeant Pizzo was acutely aware of city police officer's opinion of him. He wasn't liked. Even the other commanders disliked him. He was brash and unfriendly at work, and drunk off duty.

We had mutual friends: Gus, Angelo, and Carmen Lombardo, the restaurant guys. The focal point of the Walnut Park Neighborhood. They apparently told Phil Pizzo to look after me, or take care of me, or mentor me. Something not wanted or needed. He was apparently in the bloody ninth awaiting promotion to lieutenant. He had no platoon of cops to lead, so he was a relief supervisor, wandering around and filling in for supervisors who were on vacation or sick leave.

For some unknown reason strangers think young cops need protection, or a godfather, or Rabbi to help them. Being self-sufficient is part of the survival process in a big city police department.

Friends of friends (outside influence) packs a lot of weight in the decision-making process within the department. It's one of the things wrong with the system here. Some cops rely on outside influence for the entire careers; promotions, transfers, choice of partners.

The recipient becomes spoiled by the system. A city cop should be able to handle himself/herself, under almost any circumstances, without an ace. Phil Pizzo was super friendly to the cop/writer, and his concern was appreciated, but not needed.

The bloody ninth district had been my work/home for approximately a year when Sergeant Pizzo showed up there. He started asking about me, and eventually introduced himself. My Platoon Sergeant at the time was Bill Vorbeck. He advised me to stay clear of Phil Pizzo. That was my intent. My watch Commander was Lieutenant Bob Scheetz; he ordered Phil Pizzo to stay away from me.

Sergeant Pizzo began his indoctrination of the cop/writer and Glen Vaughn. "James Leroy Cochran has abducted another person, a Florissant resident, John Dorrell III. He went to a doctor's appointment and never made it back home. Cochran allowed him to call his wife. No telling where he is, but odds have it he's going to be coming back to Walnut Park, or Baden. He's riding around in the guy's car, with the hostage. It's a red 1970

Plymouth Barracuda, a fast sports type car. Tonight, you two are going to be detailed in the sixth district, looking for him and the hostage. If you see him, kill him. Shoot him with those shotguns and make certain he's dead."

"He's got a hostage, right?" Cop/writer muttered. "What if the hostage gets in the line of fire?"

This isn't a perfect scenario, officer," he said. "Everyone living in Walnut Park and Baden knows this asshole. He's been trouble since he was born. He was never violent, but people change. He's now a mad dog, and he's wounded. You do what you have-to do to put this asshole down. You took an oath when you were hired on, remember? To protect the people and property of the citizens of the State of Missouri and the City of St. Louis. Walnut Park and Baden are my neighborhoods. I live there. You live there, too. You're excused!"

We walked to our car without speaking. We had our shotguns on our shoulders, like two kids going duck hunting. The cop/writer slid into the driver's seat and Glen rode shotgun. We had the big and bogus shotguns between us in the front seat, muzzles to the floor. We steered down North Grand to North Broadway, and then turned north toward Baden. We hadn't spoken, yet.

We cruised around the gigantic Bellefontaine and Calvary Cemeteries, and noticed other cops patrolling the same perimeter.

"So, are you mentally prepared to kill this goofy bank robber?"

"No," Glen quickly replied as if he was waiting for question. "Jimmy Cochran is a barking dog. He's shot at some police cars, but he's never hit anybody with his shots. He's just signifying. He's a glory hound who can't get enough of himself."

We cruised, Glen paused, and then started again. "Do you know who Phil Pizzo is?"

Cops make mental dossiers on almost every cop they come into contact with; mine wasn't to be shared with Glen Vaughn. "No," cop/writer replied. "A supervisor in the police department who gave us an order to kill someone? Is that uncommon?"

"Phil Pizzo is a drunk police commander who has never made an arrest in his life," Glen began. "He's a politician; he makes rank because he's friends with other politicians. He's a fifty-year old man and he lives with his mommy, at her house, in Walnut Park. He's a relief sergeant, which means the department heads won't give him a platoon of cops to command. He's not worthy of leading, so they'll just pass him around to the southern districts, and he'll go to rollcall and berate the cops who do all of the work, ride around for eight hours and then go home to his mommy. He's here awaiting a promotion to lieutenant. Then, the chief's office will have to figure out where to hide him within the police department, so he won't embarrass the chief."

"Oh, I didn't know that," cop/writer lied.

Glen continued to take the bait. "He's got a brother in the second district, the tamest and slowest district in the city He's got rank, too. He's a sergeant. You know what his job is?"

"No!"

"He parks cars for rich people at the Municipal Opera. A fucking police sergeant. The rich park their cars illegally in or near the front door of the opera and go inside without telling anyone about their deal with this sergeant. They leave cash on the dashboard, or on the seat, and Phil's brother goes by and collects the cash.

This occurs every night during the Muny season. He's making a killing."

Driving in the darkness and musing in amazement on how city cops know the intricacies of their comrades in arms.

"Phil Pizzo has a lot of nerve telling us to go out to another district and kill some asshole bank robber, while he's sitting in the district station drinking coffee, or looking at some girly magazine, or sitting on the commode. It's the biggest joke in showbusiness."

Another prime example of the two ideologies clashing. Cops who investigate and work to arrest criminals, and cop politicians out to make more rank. There was a lesson to be learned with this barrage of information provided by Glen Vaughn. Reader/friend, do you think this "wanna be" hero/detective used this information to his advantage? He did not!

We cruised in the sixth district, around the cemeteries, up and down Riverview Boulevard, and down toward the Mississippi River on Riverview Drive. At approximately 0100, the police dispatcher alerted all city cars that James Leroy Cochran was headed east on I-270 from Florissant Road, and that he would be at Riverview Drive and I-270 in approximately three minutes.

We were on Riverview Drive. The floored, sick, old, and worn-out scout car shuttered and stuttered, as we raced toward the intersection of Riverview Drive and I-270. The excitement was building, and the peer pressure was mounting. St. Louis cops were famous for killing bad guys; murder for $8,000 a year was the muse of the moment.

"What's the plan?"

"I'm not shooting into the car," Glen replied. "If we do, we will kill the hostage. There's something I gotta tell you."

"What?"

"John Dorrell the third is my neighbor. He's a friend of mine and I don't want him injured."

It was time to devise a plan,

"Okay," cop/writer replied. "I'll take the front tires and you take the rear tires. With these shotguns we should be able to blow the wheels right off the Barracuda. Whatever happens after that, we'll just play it by ear."

"If we do that, Cochran is going to crash the car, on the bridge leading over the Mississippi River," Glen Vaughn replied. "There's guardrails, but not good ones. He's gonna be traveling at a fast clip. I'm not shooting at the car!"

Quick thoughts, again, "Okay, me neither, but we gotta make it look good in case anyone else shows up at the river."

We drove up onto the entrance ramp to I-270 right before the highway turns into the bridge that goes over the Mississippi River. The confluence of the Mississippi and the Missouri is just a quarter mile north. I had a brief thought about Lewis and Clark, the explorers who charted the two rivers. They may have camped here. Now two cops are colluding to disobey an order from a political supervisor, cop commander, to shoot a bank robber here; and probably end the life of a hostage.

We got out of the scout car and waited, with our shotguns shouldered and ready. We were both cool as cucumbers, as if we were two kids playing cops and robbers. It was too easy; the information was too relevant to be true. It couldn't be true, but it was.

James Leroy Cochran zoomed by us at about ninety. My shotgun was aimed right at his head, but the trigger was not pulled. The hostage stared at us as they whizzed by. It was over in an instant. Had we pulled the triggers it would have never been over; we wouldn't have been heroes; we would have been murderers.

We cruised the remainder of the night. There wasn't much more chatter from Glen. The ride in the darkness, John Dorrell III, the Mississippi River Bridge had just about taken everything out of him that was available for this night watch ride in the people factory. We made relief and Sergeant Pizzo was waiting for us.

"Did you two go to the intersection of I-270 and Riverview Drive?"

"Yes, sir," I replied. James Leroy Cochran didn't come by us. We were waiting for him. The information must've been bogus." Glen didn't look at Sergeant Pizzo. During our conversations with him Glen never uttered a word or gave him a look. The cop ideologies were so deeply seated, it was frightening.

 John Dorrell's wife (hostage) had a day and a night filled with anxiety. While she was speaking to her husband on the telephone, Jimmy Cochran grabbed the receiver and advised Mrs. Dorrell that her husband would not be harmed. The FBI was listening to the telephone conversation. They tried to trace the call but failed. Two days went by and there was no further contact by Dorrell.

Jimmy Cochran eventually released Dorrell in Jennings, a north county municipality attached to Walnut Park, near Lombardo's Restaurant. Dorrell said the trip to Albuquerque was paid for by using Dorrell's credit card. Cochran took $40.00 from Dorrell, but eventually paid him back $15.00, and told him he would repay him at some point. Jimmy abandoned Dorrell's 1970 Plymouth Barracuda in the 1200 block of Ann Avenue, in south city, near the brewery. He was back in the city and working his way back to Baden, and Walnut park.

Jimmy was to the point of seeking help from friends. He went to the home of an old friend and asked for help. The friend took him in, fed him, gave him his Pontiac Station Wagon, and $5.00, and called the police after Jimmy left his home.

Jimmy tried to force his way into another north city home. The lady living there called the police. The responding officers observed Jimmy running away from the house, and they pursued him. They lost sight of him when he ran into Calvary Cemetery. Again, home free in his home graveyard. The city cops roamed Calvary but didn't locate him. Jimmy was like a Badger in a den.

The following day the search shifted to Columbus, Ohio. Four members of a Hillsboro, Missouri family (south of St. Louis in Jefferson County) were abducted by Jimmy, held captive and forced to drive to Columbus. One of the victims was a twenty-four-year-old Army Sergeant. His wife, and her parents were in the house when the sergeant came home to the hostage event. Jimmy told them he wanted to get cleaned up, eat and leave after dark.

They allowed Jimmy to take a bath, shave, and tend to his bullet wounds. His left arm was turning dark brown, and was continually bleeding. He had pock marks on his back where the buckshot from the shotguns hit when he was running away from the city cops.

Luckily for him, he had on a heavy jacket when they fired on him. The buckshot was fired from a long distance and didn't break the skin. The folks from Hillsboro cooked fried chicken for Jimmy, with the trimmings, and they all ate a great dinner, like family folk.

At dark, they all piled into the sergeant's 1971 Plymouth and headed east. Jimmy rode in the backseat while the sergeant drove. Part of the time Jimmy had the pistol pointed at the sergeant. Jimmy told them he wanted to go to Richmond, Indiana, near the Ohio state line, but when they arrived there, he wanted to continue on. During the trip, Jimmy warned the sergeant not to speed or direct any attention to them. Jimmy let the family out of the car in Columbus near a bus station.

Jimmy telephoned his Leavenworth buddy, Scotty, when they got to Columbus. The FBI had already been to Scotty's residence. They told Scotty to contact them if Jimmy contacted him. He warned Jimmy to stay away, and that he should probably turn himself in. Jimmy was running out of options.

Jimmy had changed clothing after the bath at the house in Hillsboro, and was now armed with two pistols and a high-powered rifle he had taken from the Hillsboro house. He had warned the sergeant and his family that if they didn't cooperate with him, he would kill them all.

Jimmy had been telephoning his girlfriend periodically from the houses of his hostages. He knew the FBI was listening and trying to trace his calls. He told her he was tired of running and he was in great pain from his gunshot wounds. She pleaded with Jimmy to give himself up.

He told one of the FBI agents at his girlfriend's house that he was at a Holiday Inn in Lexington, Kentucky. He gave the agent the address and told him he was registered under his own name, and that he was unarmed.

FBI agents converged on the motel, and called Jimmy's room on the house telephone. They had the motel surrounded; they ordered Jimmy to come out of his room with his hands up. Jimmy refused to come out. He told them he was unarmed and had just gotten out of the shower, and was nude. Jimmy figured they would shoot him if he came out of his room.

Jimmy opened the motel room door and fifteen FBI agents burst inside. Jimmy stood there with his hands in the air, nude. It's difficult to murder a nude man; self-defense is not an option. Jimmy counted the agents and smiled at them. They ordered him to get dressed. An agent got verbally nasty with him. Jimmy wasn't resisting or causing any problems; he was just dressing. They shackled Jimmy and made the decision to use a handcuff to attach him to an agent so Jimmy couldn't run from them when they got outside. Jimmy said, "shackle me to him," pointing at the agent who had verbally abused him. They did.

Agents found the 1971 Plymouth Jimmy had taken from the Hillsboro, Missouri family parked near the motel. They found two pistols and a high-powered rifle inside.

Jimmy was taken to Good Samaritan Hospital in Lexington. He seemed relaxed, relieved. He joked with the doctors and the nurses. Jimmy had done what he wanted to do: gain notoriety, vengeance, and be on the minds of every person in the country; he was James Leroy Cochran from Baden; bank robber, abductor, fugitive and all-around-good-guy.

He was treated and taken to the Fayette County, Kentucky Jail. The next morning, he was taken before United States Magistrate G. Murray Smith Jr., who fixed his bail at $100,000.

But Jimmy had other problems. The blue Pontiac he used to rob the bank, the car Jimmy incinerated, following the instructions on the note in the car; the one with the .38 caliber pistol in the glove box; it belonged to his cop friend's wife, Marilyn Oliver. Marilyn Oliver was now a missing person. The cops and the FBI suspected Jimmy had murdered her.

8

At about 5:30 that same afternoon, a farmer had gone to an abandoned farmhouse near Leslie, Missouri, about seventy-five miles west of the City of St. Louis. The house hadn't been used for years, but the farmer had used it as a warehouse to store feed and farm equipment, and he had gone to the house to pick up some corn.

He walked to the rear of the house and as he started up onto the porch his attention was directed to some large feed sacks on the porch. Protruding from under the burlap bags was a foot. He also noticed some dark spots that looked like blood. He called the Franklin County Sheriff's Office.

A deputy responded, "I didn't touch a thing after I saw that foot," the farmer advised him. There was a female body under the burlap bags, apparently shot in the torso, at least five times. The body was badly decomposed. The deputy had a hunch that the body was that of Marilyn Oliver.

The major case squad had been called in after Marilyn's car had been used by Jimmy to rob the bank, after she was reported missing. The theory was Jimmy had murdered her, or had her tied up in an apartment somewhere in Baden.

Major Robert Lowery, head of the Major Case Squad in St. Louis, was contacted, He and his detectives responded, set up lights, and investigated the scene. The body was clad in a red blouse, and dark slacks. The jewelry on the body was the same type reported in the missing person's report.

The body was conveyed to a St. Louis County hospital; the detectives continued searching the farmhouse. Sergeant Noser, Major Lowery' assistant, found an expended shell casing on the porch. The next morning the medical examiner reported the woman had been shot six-tines and had been dead about ten days. Pinpointing the time of death was considered of great importance in the case, so insect life taken from the corpse was sent to the Biology Department of St. Louis University for examination.

As the investigation of the farmhouse and the corpse continued, investigators formed a pattern of the crime. It appeared Marilyn Oliver was shot inside the farmhouse, and then shot several more times as she staggered outside to the porch. Blood spattering on the walls and door marked her route of death.

City of St. Louis Police Officer, Patrolman Bill Oliver, Marilyn's estranged husband, had responded to the farmhouse crime scene and made a positive identification of the corpse. He stated he had seen her wearing the slacks and blouse, many times, and that the jewelry she was wearing was his wife's.

He again said he saw Marilyn wearing that outfit many times. True investigators pick up on statements like the one Bill Oliver made. It's the difference from the beat cop and the investigator. Beat cops are amateurs.

Back in the federal jail in Lexington, Kentucky, Jimmy had been given the news about the deceased Marilyn Oliver, and that he was a suspect in her murder. Jimmy wasn't feeling like a hero from Baden, anymore.

He had asked to speak to a United States Marshall, and he professed his innocence regarding the Marilyn Oliver murder. The crime, the chase, the hiding and shooting and abducting; they were all just fun and games to James Leroy Cochran. The fun and games were over. Jimmy could get the death penalty.

The weapons found inside the last car Jimmy stole from one of his hostages, and the especially the .38 caliber Smith & Wesson pistol, were of great importance to the investigators. City cops were only allowed to carry a Smith & Wesson .38, or a Colt .38. City cops couldn't even carry a different brand or caliber weapon off duty. The police department issued Smith & Wesson .38s as the duty weapon. They were heavy, with four-inch barrels and difficult to conceal.

Many of the cops desired, and purchased .357 magnum Smith & Wesson, or Colt pistols with six-inch barrels to carry on duty. The department allowed them to do so, but they weren't allowed to load them with .357 ammunition. They were forced to load them with department issued .38 ammo.

The big stainless, or chrome Smith & Wesson's, and Colt Pythons were beautiful weapons, but damned expensive. The cops who purchased and carried them on duty also had to cover the expense of a new leather holsters and gun belts. It was all about show for the beat cops.

At rollcall, the precinct sergeant would shout "prepare for inspection." We would all stand in a line with our guns drawn, held up by our faces, and the sarge would go by and inspect us for cleanliness, sobriety, and attitude, and then order us to unload our weapons; looking for .357 ammo.

Every time this occurred (which was often), cops would say to themselves, "is this where I belong?" Most of us carried the attitude that we were above all of this petty inspection of the ammo ritual. If we were past military, we felt we'd had enough of the gun culture to make us experts for a lifetime. Add to the fact that the federal government was paying us to go to college, off-duty, and we felt above everything and everyone, pertaining to orders and discipline.

The problem with the .357 ammo was, that the projectile was of such velocity, it would go through a body and go into another person's body, maybe more than one other person's body. The bullet just kept on going. If that other body was a cop, (maybe a partner) then there would be a dead cop the watch commander would have to explain about to a grieving wife.

But the beat cops knew how to get around the .357 ammo dilemma. They would load their own ammo and place a "hot charge" in the regular department shell casing. The "hot load" would be almost as strong as the .357 load, but it would look just like a department bullet.

Cop/writer found all of this skullduggery over weapons and bullets mind boggling. Cop/writer carried the old department .38 four-inch barreled Smith & Wesson. The projectiles that struck Jimmy Cochran as he ran from the police, or in the shootout on Riverview Boulevard near Northwest High School, were either .357 magnums or "hot loads".

From a distance of more than sixty feet, the .38 loses its velocity and begins tumbling. The bullets that struck Jimmy weren't tumbling, and they were fired from a long distance.

The .38 is a belly gun, meaning it is good for short distances, such as inside of someone's apartment or house, where cops go all day or all night trying to keep the peace. Or for cops like cop/writer and Tom Rangel to shoot into windshields of rapist's Cadillacs.

The .38 caliber Smith & Wesson pistol found in the last hostage's car was sent to the FBI laboratory for testing. They compared the pistol ballistics to the bullets found in Marilyn Oliver's corpse. They matched. It was the gun that killed Marilyn Oliver. So, Jimmy was driving and robbing a bank with Marilyn Oliver's car, and he used, and was in possession of the gun used to murder her.

Jimmy was wondering if it was the proper time to contact his criminal defense attorney, and friend, Norm London. Jimmy had no money. He'd have to wait it out. For guys like Jimmy, and Norm London, it isn't a crime to be a criminal; the crime begins when one gets caught. And even after the crook is arrested, it doesn't exactly mean he, or she, is a criminal.

The alleged crook could've been misidentified; the cops could have framed or cased him; the forensics could be wrong. And, even if the crook is convicted in a court of law, and deemed guilty by a jury of his, or hers, peers, it doesn't mean, precisely, that the defendant is a criminal.

This is the free enterprise system. In America, we are free to pursue happiness in any way we desire, unless there's a victim, such as Marilyn Oliver.

Free enterprise stops at murder. It's a game of cat and mouse; a chess game for not smart crooks (ones who get caught), and for smart crooks like Norm London to represent them in court.

Norm never got caught, but he was snitched on in federal court, in the Southern District of Illinois, by a snitch defendant, Rick Yackey. Seems Norm ponied up $100,000 for an investment in a marijuana smuggling scheme. His good friend, Dan Robinson (a criminal, pimp, drug dealer, who hung out in Norm's office) was in cahoots with his brother, the notorious Paul Robinson, (killer, pimp, smuggler) and professional convict. Norm was supposed to get a 100% profit on his investment within six months. Paul Robinson stiffed him; Norm got nothing.

When a caught criminal hires a defense lawyer, the first thing the attorney asks the defendant is, "What do they say you did?" Jimmy and Norm were as thick as thieves. Norm never got caught because he didn't want to be caught. James Leroy Cochran, deep down inside of his psyche, wanted to be caught. The notoriety is all he thinks about, even though he touts revenge, and his dad's accidental drowning. We all die, one way or another.

Jimmy's gotten away with other armed robberies; why desire revenge for the one he didn't do. I've heard cop detectives brag about "casing", or "framing" career criminals. "Maybe he didn't do this one, but he's done a hundred other heinous crimes," they would say. The detective feels honor bound, obligated, to incarcerate career criminals. They are duty bound. Lying in court, state or federal, does not affect them.

For the true criminal, the guy, or gal who devotes his life to being a criminal, time in incarceration, somewhat, is a vacation for him, particularly federal incarceration. He can reflect and regroup. It doesn't mean he's a bad guy, or a monster (although many are) it just means they're ornery and misguided. They all feel they will get out of prison some day; they just wait it out.

Some criminals are so incensed with money, that they can think of nothing but making, or stealing it. It's like a sex offender obsessed with sex, or a drunk obsessed with booze. The history of America is based on criminals getting what they want by stealing or taking it at gunpoint, especially the robbing of banks, the worst way for a criminal to make money. The pay is bad, (in most instances) and the deed is dangerous.

But in the minds of the public, law abiding, go to work and come home to the family for supper types, banks are the bad-guys, and some of the bank robbers are the good-guys. Look at how Jimmy's abductees treated him. He walked into their homes, threatened them with a pistol, and held them hostage. They cooked for him, allowed him to take a bath, talked and drank with him.

Jimmy wasn't the government, changing their neighborhoods, forcing them to leave their homes and find a new place to live, safe from hatred. He wasn't the bank repossessing their family car, or their family house. Who's the bad-guy? James Leroy Cochran is a friendly guy, and a good guy to talk with. I can see why Norm London, rich and powerful criminal defense lawyer would like him.

"Tell the cops where you got the car and the gun," Norm would advise Jimmy (when he eventually visited him in jail.)

"No," Jimmy would reply. "I swore I wouldn't do it, and I won't."

"I can get the court to incarcerate you on an insanity plea," Norm would say.

"Never," Jimmy would reply. Jimmy wasn't criminally insane; he was just nuts. There has to be something mentally wrong with someone who desires to be incarcerated just to get one's name in the paper, or to prove a point.

Norm knew what Jimmy's response would be, and he knew how to work around the "code of silence", professed by every crook, and cop, and defense attorney, but seldom adhered to. Jimmy stuck to the code. He and Norm figured the current investigation would clear him of the murder.

Jimmy had boasted to several of his hostages that he had killed before. It was false bravado on Jimmy's behest. Somehow, a hostage, or a cop, or an FBI agent misconstrued Jimmy's statement, and it came out that Jimmy bragged about killing a woman.

This type of misinformation is deadly to the crook, and in some cases allows the real perpetrator to go free. It's why there are Norm London's in the crook/cop game. Smart people can ferret out false information. It changes the minds and attitudes of the jury, and many times brings a judgement of "not guilty."

One misinformative statement, detected by a good lawyer, can change the outcome of a criminal trial. The FBI and Major Lowery of the Florissant Police Department, and the head of the major Case Squad, interviewed the hostages. They all told the investigators that Jimmy treated them well, and that when Jimmy rambled about his past criminal experiences, they figured he was just trying to control them. In the meantime, Jimmy requested a lie detector test.

This cop/writer had been around the Jimmy's and the Norm's of this world for decades. His home-town is East St. Louis, Illinois. Desperate people came from all over the United States to come to his other metro east home town (Alton, Illinois) to work at the factories. Many were criminals and they brought their criminal children with them. They were his classmates in grade school, junior high school, and high school.

It wasn't difficult to form a hypothesis early in life: ten percent of the people one meets, deals with, converses with on a daily basis are hardened criminals, mentally capable of ending your life. Ten percent are just regular crooks; thieves, pimps, fences, people who would do anything for money. And another ten percent are people who are always looking for a way to cheat someone; friends, relatives, associates.

A third of the population are out to get you. (This hypothesis kept this cop/writer alive and un-incarcerated through four years in the United States Marine Corps, and thirty-five years as a big-city cop.)

And, in the minds of Jimmy, and Norm London, cops are as culpable as crooks. Jurors don't always believe cops. Some jurors hate cops and wouldn't believe anything they testify to. Cops lie, just like defendants. They lie from peer pressure. They desire to satisfy their bosses, and they want to be seen as staunch crime fighters. A super good lawyer like Norm London can spot a lying cop in a heartbeat. Norm has the ability to make the jurors identify dishonesty in a cop or a witness. Norm was going to get James Leroy Cochran, his buddy, leniency.

Franklin County Prosecuting Attorney Daniel M. Buescher announced in Union, Missouri that Jimmy had been charged with first degree murder in the slaying of Marilyn Oliver. The incriminating evidence in the case was the .38 caliber Smith & Wesson revolver used to murder Marilyn Oliver, which was found in the abandoned car owned by one of the hostages of Jimmy's rampage of fame.

Nobody ever told Jimmy that "fame was fleeting", like dry ice; cool for a while and then it's gone, and nobody remembers what it was. Jimmy was taken from Kentucky to St. Louis and housed in a federal facility, awaiting trial on state and federal charges.

Jimmy had other problems relating to the Marilyn Oliver murder; his bank robbing partner, Paul L. Lockhart, had relatives with a farm next to the farmhouse where Marilyn Oliver's body was found.

It is circumstantial evidence, at the very least, which means nothing to anyone on the surface, but in the minds of a jury it shows connection to a crime. People have been stoned, hanged, burned, electrocuted, and gassed due to circumstantial evidence since "an eye for an eye" was considered justice.

So, the case against Jimmy Cochran was: the .38 Smith & Wesson used to kill Marilyn Oliver; that he was associated with Marilyn Oliver and had seen her socially in the recent past, and the fact that he had told his hostages he had killed a woman, which was an untrue statement.

During the interviews by Major Lowery of the Major Case Squad, Jimmy allegedly told his hostages he shot the woman five times, in the head. Marilyn Oliver was shot six times in the body. There wasn't one shot in her head.

Major Lowery noted that there were some things in the case that didn't add up. Jimmy gave himself up in Lexington, Kentucky, but left the murder weapon in the hostage vehicle, parked nearby. Major Lowery met with Lieutenant Norman Jacobsmeyer of the City of St. Louis Homicide Section. They exchanged ideas about the Marilyn Oliver murder.

Lieutenant Jacobsmeyer informed Major Lowery about a statement made by a girlfriend of Patrolman Bill

Oliver regarding Marilyn Oliver. Patrolman Oliver allegedly met this woman on a routine call concerning a stolen auto. They became friends and began dating. Not long into their friendship, Patrolman Oliver stated to her that if there was any way he could get rid of his wife, he'd do it.

She also advised that a few days after Marilyn's body was found Patrolman, Oliver again came to her apartment; they had a lover's quarrel and Oliver threatened her. "If you snitch on me, I'll take care of you like I did my wife."

Major Lowery wondered why Patrolman Oliver, or anyone who had just committed a murder, would make an incriminating statement to a lover, or friend. Was Oliver trying to impress this woman? Was this a made-up story by an angry lover? Those were question's the Major Case Squad would have to address.

Major Lowery and his squad began interviewing friends and relatives of Marilyn Oliver. They came up with the same answers after every interview: Patrolman Bill Oliver was capable of anything and would do anything for money.

He had stated to a relative of Marilyn's that he left her car in a parking lot behind a business on North Broadway with the keys in it so it would be stolen, and he could collect the insurance money. Marilyn was spending nights at friend's houses because she was afraid of Bill Oliver. Although she told the same friends that she would go back with him, if he asked her.

One woman interviewed by Major Lowery advised them that Marilyn told her that if anything happened to her, it was her husband who did it. She was in love with her husband, but he was running around on her, and beating her badly.

Oliver had picked up his wife's paycheck at her place of employment, prior to the discovery of her body. He also checked on her life insurance policy. The investigators went to a home of a woman who was friends with Marilyn Oliver. Marilyn had advised her she was pregnant and had informed Bill Oliver about it. Bill Oliver became upset about the pregnancy. It was going to cost him money.

Patrolman Bill Oliver was apparently a business and residence burglar, and his wife, Marilyn Oliver, knew about his extracurricular ways to make extra money. Marilyn had enough evidence on Bill Oliver to burn him, and she was contemplating going to his commanding officer and informing on him.

The investigators asked the woman if she thought Bill Oliver murdered Marilyn Oliver. Marilyn loved Bill Oliver and would have gone anywhere with him; even to a farmhouse to be killed.

The investigators went to the federal lockup of the St. Louis City Jail to interview Jimmy Cochran. Jimmy talked freely. They again asked Jimmy where he got the .38 Smith & Wesson pistol, and Marilyn's car. Again, Jimmy told the investigators that he called a person he knew and told him he needed a car and a gun, and arrangements were made to pick up the car behind a store in a mall on North Broadway.

The gun was in the glove box, with the note stating Jimmy should burn the car, but bring the gun back to him. Jimmy paid the person $500.00. Jimmy again refused to name the person. In his mind, naming the co-conspirator would be more of a crime than serving the time for a murder he didn't commit.

It is remarkable how captured criminals have the ability to separate and classify their past crimes. It is almost brilliant how these not bright individuals can regurgitate their assault against society, or working stiffs; the sordid criminal acts languish in their psyche waiting to be tapped at their will. But the criminal's jaundiced rationale is insignificant. No one cares how a crook's criminal past is dissected, even his defense attorney.

Jimmy again stated he wanted a polygraph test, and his request was granted. A polygraph test was given to Jimmy, three times. He passed the test.

The investigators turned their attention to the type of ammunition that was in the gun when Jimmy obtained it. They were 158 grain .38 hollow-points of a brand, named Norma. They are the kind the St. Louis Police use and issue. It is unusual that a holdup man, one who doesn't even own a car, would buy these types of bullets.

The investigators started a tour of gun stores and sporting stores that carried ammunition, and they eventually came to a gun store in Pagedale, a north St. Louis County municipality. They searched the records of the sales of ammunition and discovered that Patrolman Bill Oliver had purchased a box of Norma .38s, a few months before the murder of Marilyn Oliver, and the robbery of the Cass Savings and Loan.

The investigators decided to interview Patrolman Bill Oliver. He told the investigators that his wife had a boyfriend, and that he (Bill Oliver) had gone to Marilyn's apartment one evening and noticed a bottle of Scotch and two empty glasses on a table, and the bed messed up.

It was a stupid lie, because both of the investigators had gone to the apartment on the same night in question, and did not see a Scotch bottle, or a messed-up bed. Stupid people tell stupid lies.

The case on Jimmy Cochran was falling apart. The case against Patrolman Bill Oliver for the murder of his wife, Marilyn Oliver, was forming. Another stupid lie: the red blouse and slacks Marilyn was wearing when she was murdered were purchased shortly before her death. A relative of Marilyn's was with her when she purchased them. Bill Oliver had never seen them. At the murder scene, Bill Oliver stated he recognized the blouse and slacks, and he had seen her wearing them often.

Another stupid lie: In an earlier interview with police, Oliver had said he was on duty the Thursday of the Savings and Loan robbery, and he heard a radio report, and feared his wife's car might have been used.

Bill Oliver said he heard the description of the car, and the license plate number. He said he had seen the license plate number many times. The investigators established a timeline of when the plates were purchased, which was just before Marilyn went missing, and were installed onto her car by a St. Louis City cop, friend of Marilyn's.

The .38 Smith & Wesson used to kill Marilyn was unique in several ways; it was chrome plated, had pearl handles, and one of the handles was broken. Investigators were told by numerous people they had seen such a weapon in Patrolman Bill Oliver's possession.

As the investigation deepened, rumors ran rampant through the St. Louis Police Department. Cops were coming out of the woodwork to give information on their crooked cop associate. One cop told the investigators that he had stopped Bill Oliver for speeding and noticed that he had the .38 Smith & Wesson with pearl handles, one broken, in his waist band.

Major Lowery studied the massive amount of information his investigators had dug up. The information was taken to Prosecuting Attorney Daniel M. Bueschler in Union, Missouri. Subsequently, the murder charge against James Leroy Cochran was dismissed, and like charges were filed against Patrolman William C. Oliver.

Patrolman Oliver's trial was moved to Phelps County on a change of venue. The trial lasted a week; evidence gathered by the investigators of the Major Case Squad was presented. The jury was out for four hours, then came in with a verdict of second-degree murder. They gave Bill Oliver twenty-five years.

I know what you are asking yourselves, reader/friend. Did Patrolman Bill Oliver set-up Jimmy Cochran with the gun and the car? Did Bill Oliver base his murder of his wife on the chance that Jimmy Cochran would blindly go into Cass Savings and loan, rob it, burn Marilyn's car and then shoot it out with the cops and hopefully get killed by them. Dead men tell no tales.

Had Jimmy been killed by the sixth district cops, or by Patrolman (ex-detective) Glen Vaughn, and this cop/writer, there wouldn't have been a Major Case Squad investigation. It would have been cut and dried. Jimmy the gentle bank robber would have been buried in his favorite cemetery and forgotten about. The .38 Smith & Wesson would have clinched the dead bank robber's guilt.

I think, friend/reader, you are also asking yourself if the cop who was robbing heroin dealers in the bloody ninth district, and sometimes shooting them, was

Patrolman Bill Oliver? Jimmy knows the answer to both of those questions, but Jimmy isn't talking.

There's irony in the cop game, reader/friend, (anyone who reads this cop/writer's books is a true friend.) In the cop business there's joy, sorrow, horror, and redemption, and that's usually in one eight-hour shift. It is the greatest show on earth.

An update on Phil Pizzo: Phil was promoted to Lieutenant and stayed in the bloody ninth district for a short time. He was eventually moved to the Hampton Avenue District. Phil was drinking, off-duty, in a bar in west St. Louis County and met a couple, the Querys, (David and Virginia) who were also drinking. They invited Phil to their apartment to play cards. What's the harm? Phil was a nice guy, and he was a commander in the St. Louis Metropolitan Police Department. Vlad the Impaler was going to be their house guest and card playing partner. Phil accepted the invitation.

The drinking and the card game lasted all night. Phil and the Querys began arguing, and Phil apparently damaged some furniture, and pointed his pistol at them. Mrs. Query called the police to have Phil removed from their home.

Somehow, a camera news crew got word about a City of St. Louis Police Lieutenant was destroying furniture and flourishing his pistol and they accompanied the St. Louis County Officer (female) to the Query's home. Phil was out of control and he struck the county officer on her arm and shoulder. He was so intoxicated that he looked like a madman, and all of this was on the evening news.

Phil was arrested for assaulting the county police officer and for destroying furniture inside of the Query's house. Phil had done what the prima donnas in the ivory tower (chief's office) had hoped he would not do. He embarrassed them. Lieutenant Phil Pizzo was suspended.

Phil eventually got his job back. He was the laughingstock of the police department; most cops, young and old avoided him. In the headquarters building, where the elite and not so elite meet and greet, Phil was accosted by young cops who had learned to despise him for his caustic demeanor. They knew Phil's Achilles Heel. Some would ask him incriminating questions, like, "Hey Lieutenant, you got that drinking problem taken care of?"

Or, "Hey Lieutenant, I saw you on the evening news, keep up the good work."

Or, "Hey Lieutenant, I heard you're going to have your own television series, The Drunk Lieutenant Show, starring Phil Pizzo."

Or, "Lieutenant Pizzo, you still hitting the bottle?"

Phil would turn and snap at them, "It's none of your fucking business what I do, officer." Phil was always prepared to scrap to protect his self-imposed image.

Phil retired and didn't last long. He had moved his momma out of Walnut Park to a nice home in south St. Louis County where they both lived. The demographic change of the Walnut Park was devasting to all its inhabitants. She outlasted him.

Glen Vaughn resigned from the police department. He went to Colorado to be a deputy sheriff in a small community there in the mountains. He couldn't get over the murder, before his very eyes, of his friend and fellow warrior, Detective Mel Wilmoth. Glen was haunted by the images of instant shock, turmoil, panic, and death.

The place in Colorado, as he described it, seemed like paradise. He didn't mention his wife and two kids. He had a small house in Florissant, (north St. Louis County), and from our conversation, his wife and he were estranged, and that she and the kids were going to stay in Florissant.

Glen wasn't gone long, and he was asking for his job back in the St. Louis Police Department. The job here spoils us. At that point in time, cops could do almost anything and get away with it, murder, driving drunk, assault, you name it, a St. Louis cop could do, if he was savvy enough to be able to explain his actions on paper. Most were. Some were not, Phil Pizzo and Bill Oliver, to name a few.

Glen got his job back. The city was begging for police officers. It was the hippy revolution, and the tail end of the Viet Nam War. Cops were being drafted and men, and women in their twenties didn't want to be cops. Glen was back in the blue riding around in a north city district, collecting a paycheck and living back with his wife and kids.

Fast forward to 1986, this cop/writer was assigned to the Intelligence Unit investigating organized criminals and loving it. Glen Vaughn was still in a north district. He was celebrating his 48th birthday at a home in the 2800 block of Montgomery (bad neighborhood), with a friend, William J. Huff.

Glen and his friend decided to go outside and fire their revolvers into the air as part of the celebration. They did so, and neighbors called the police. Penrose District Officers Phelps and James Conner responded to the area of 10th and Montgomery at about 12:30 a.m. They heard a gunshot and observed Huff of the back porch with a revolver in his hand.

Phelps and Conner identified themselves as police officers and told Huff to drop his weapon. Huff fired a shot at them. The officers returned fire, and Huff, who was not hit, ran through a back door. Conner went to the front of the house while Phelps returned to the police car, called for assistance, and then went back to the rear of the house with a shotgun.

Huff came out of the back door and fired another shot at Phelps; Phelps fired back with the shotgun, striking Huff. Glen Vaughn then walked through the door with a revolver in his hand. Phelps took the revolver from Vaughn, and a .38 caliber pistol from Huff.

Glen Vaughn's birthday buddy, Huff, was taken to St. Louis University Hospital and admitted with wounds to his stomach, head, and legs; listed in critical condition.

Glen Vaughn was arrested and booked for unlawful use of a weapon, and being intoxicated while possessing a weapon, and discharging a weapon in the city. Huff was charged with second degree assault.

Captain Clarence Harmon, Commander of the Internal Affairs Division, suspended Glen Vaughn. But Clarence had nice things to say about him. He advised that Patrolman Vaughn had received five letters of commendation, and three in the past three years. Glen Vaughn was a hard charging cop and it is unusual for a commander to come to the aid of coppers like him. No one came forward to praise or defend Lieutenant Phil Pizzo.

Glen was probably going to be fired from the police department. Booze had taken over his life, and he was now on his own. He took an early retirement from the police department. He had twenty-three years on the job, which qualified him for forty-three percent of his base pay. People on welfare get paid more.

Glen didn't last long. He died a young man.

9

Jimmy Cochran was sitting in the federal section of the St. Louis City Jail, the lowest of all jails in the United States of America. He was told by a guard that he had a visitor; Jimmy asked him who it was, and the guard told him it was his lawyer.

Jimmy, as far as he was concerned, didn't have a lawyer, because he didn't have any money. He figured it was a court appointed lawyer, so Jimmy accompanied the guard to a room within the jail, walked in and observed his old friend Norm London. Norm was a welcome sight to Jimmy. Norm was super expensive, so they exchanged accolades, and Jimmy asked Norm why he was visiting him in jail.

Norm said, "Do you have $50,000?"

Jimmy replied, "No, I don't have any money."

Norm replied, "Okay, sit down here and let's see if we can get you out of this mess."

During the conversation, Norm confided in Jimmy that he had gone to the United States Attorney's office and requested to be a court appointed attorney for Jimmy. He did it because he truly liked Jimmy Cochran, bank robber, and misunderstood criminal.

But Norm London had ulterior motives: Jimmy's trial would be big publicity for whoever represented him. Norm figured he could get Jimmy a reduced sentence on the robbery of the savings and loan. But Norm had to get through the testimony of the six victims of Jimmy's abductions and hostage taking.

If he could get Jimmy off on the kidnapping charges, Jimmy could be set free in about ten years. His only defense seemed to be insanity. Jimmy was being charged with the savings and loan robbery, and three counts of kidnapping, with multiple victims.

Jimmy could have taken a plea agreement and spent the rest of his life in prison. He and Norm London had different plans. Professional criminals like Norm, and Jimmy, know that a plea is never a good idea. They decided to go to court and let a jury decide Jimmy's fate.

Although, Paul Lockhart, Jimmy's partner in the savings and loan robbery, took a plea. He got seventeen years, and Paul fired eighteen shots at the sixth district cop who was pursuing them and trying to pull them over for running a red light. Paul Lockhart gave up; he knew it was over for him. Jimmy didn't.

After Paul Lockhart entered his guilty plea and was sentenced, Paul's wife went to the United States Attorney and begged that Paul not be incarcerated in the same penitentiary as Jimmy Cochran. Her request was granted. But it seemed Paul Lockhart's fate was sealed; he was sent to the Federal Penitentiary in Marion, Illinois (super max) and was stabbed to death.

Jimmy told his acquaintances that if Paul Lockhart had been with him at Leavenworth, he would still be alive. Jimmy would have protected him. Jimmy thought Paul was a great man, and not a snitch, but he got into a knife fight during an argument; it was a knife fight that Paul lost.

.

Norm petitioned the government to have a psychiatrist examine Jimmy. There were batteries of tests and interviews before the court date. The main question law enforcement, lawyers, and judges had for Jimmy was, "Why did he do it?" He seemed to be rehabilitated, employment, girlfriend, apartment, nice clothing. What snapped inside of him to make him go back to robbing banks?

At first Jimmy used the excuse that he was acting out because his dad had been killed, drowned, in a flood while working for the railroad, right near the Mississippi River in Baden. Jimmy used that excuse for decades, and nobody cared one way or the other. It was Jimmy's life; if he wanted to spend his life behind bars, then so be it.

For the savings and loan robbery Jimmy had a different excuse for robbing banks. He referred to the ten years he did in the Missouri State Penitentiary for a robbery of a liquor store that he didn't commit. He was acting out because of that conviction. Jimmy was having rationality problems, but what criminal is rational? Jimmy's examining psychiatrist was Nathan Blackman.

As the trial evolved, Assistant United States Attorney, William C. Martin, was cross examining the psychiatrist, Nathan Blackman. It was a normal field of questions concerning the sanity of a serial bank robber, one who had also abducted and held hostage six honest, hard-working American citizens, keeping them sometimes for days.

The hostages had already testified that Jimmy treated them well, except the woman from Boonville who Jimmy had abducted, testified that Jimmy had slapped her after she became hysterical. Jimmy sat through all of this without any aggression. He knew his future was incarceration, he just didn't know how many years this last adventure in bank-robbing-land was going to cost him.

Nathan Blackman's testimony was crucial in Jimmy's defense. Norm London had done his examination of

Blackman, and it had been determined that Jimmy had problems with right and wrong, and other stupid problems and traits serial bank robbers carry around with them.

Assistant United States Attorney Martin questioned the validity of Jimmy's answers to the psychological questions Blackman had asked him. Martin brought up the possibility that Jimmy had the experience, and wherewithal, to tell Blackman what he wanted to hear, so that Blackman's evaluation of him would be positive for Jimmy in a court of law.

Blackman explained in a long statement that his judgement took into account his experience in the field of psychiatry; meaning Jimmy Cochran couldn't trick him into making him believe he was not legitimately insane.

In other words, Martin accused Jimmy of lying, or tricking Nathan Blackman. Jimmy is a crook. Crooks lie, steal, murder. The question was not out of order. Jimmy became enraged, and he began shouting at Assistant United States Attorney Martin.

Jimmy eventually went after Martin, who took refuge behind the witness stand while Jimmy was trying to get to Martin. "You calling me a liar," Jimmy shouted. Jimmy shouted some expletives about FBI agents and other cops.

It was a scary scene because Jimmy had been incarcerated for most of his life, lifting weights, sleeping, reading, knitting, crocheting, and basically eating well. Court security jumped on Jimmy and held him down. It took seven officers and an FBI agent to control him.

The outburst occurred in the seventh day of the trial, presumably the last day. The case was set to go to the jury on this afternoon. It was a prime time for Jimmy to rile up and act crazy. It was an academy award performance. I'm sure his buddy, Norm London, was proud of him. If a juror had a doubt about jimmy's sanity, Jimmy proved it to him, or her that he was indeed deranged.

The trial went to the jury, and Jimmy was convicted on the robbery of the savings and loan, but he was acquitted of the numerous kidnapping charges, probably because of his psychiatric evaluation and the violent scene in the courtroom.

Jimmy and Norm London were right in their assessment of the judicial system. Never accept a plea agreement. Always go to court and take your chances with a jury of your peers. Jimmy acts like an affable fellow, but he's a criminal just like every other criminal who walks the streets of everyone's hometown. Jimmy's just in remission.

Jimmy went away, (back to Leavenworth, his home away from home) with a twenty-five-year sentence. Flashbacks of the night with Glen Vaughn at Riverview and I-270 with our Remington shotguns pointed at Jimmy Cochran's head haunt me. All that had to be done was, lead (like hunting ducks) and squeeze the trigger. It would have been easy.

Jimmy Cochran and a bevy of St. Louis City cops are a lot alike: they have problems accepting authority; Glen Vaughn did also, although cops make their living being authority figures. Guys in the Marine Corps have authority issues, but they adjust to it. They adjust because they need employment. Jimmy adjusts to authority while he is incarcerated because he is compelled to. It's called survival. Basically, Jimmy the bank robber is a cordial guy.

Jimmy roughing it in Leavenworth, 1967. Getting in shape for his next bank robbing venture.

The hunter (author, the cop on the right), and the hunted, Jimmy Cochran, (bank robber, abductor, misunderstood crook, extraordinaire).

Jimmy and his liberal buddy, Bill McClellan, columnist for the socialist newspaper. Bill authored the nonfiction book, Evidence of Murder, touting the investigation by St. Louis homicide investigators, George Hollocher and Steve Jacobsmeyer. He is a friend to many cops.

Jimmy the bank robber after being treated for his wounds in Kentucky; he was a happy man. The escorts are two unidentified FBI agents. The conveyed him to Richmond, Kentucky for arraignment, 1971.

Jimmy, (right) and his brother Tom, also a robber, at the Missouri State Penitentiary. Referred to as "Big Jelly Roll", and "Little Jelly Roll."

Jimmy speaking with Freddy Mayer, AUSA. He prosecuted Jimmy twice for bank robbery.
They became friends. He offered to get Jimmy a presidential pardon for all of his crimes. Jimmy declined. They were meeting at Norm London's 80th birthday party.

John Dorrell III. Abducted by Jimmy Cochran; Drove with him to New Mexico. Stated Jimmy treated him well. In the car with Jimmy Cochran when Glen Vaughn and I were ordered to kill Jimmy Cochran by Lieutenant Phil Pizzo. We had 12-gauge shotguns pointed at both of them as they sped by us at 270 and Riverview Drive.

Angel Island, San Francisco Bay, scene of the Burillo boating accident.

33-foot Targa Protector assault boat, forefront, death boat.

Beautiful Lisa Castrogiovanni; Baden girl made good.

Mexican tycoon, Javier Burillo, Greg Tuck's employer and friend.

Author with my good friend, legendary badass, Greg Tuck. Wildhorse Gym. He beats up the bad-guy.

Jimmy with his good friend, Bob Kuban.

Murder victim Marilyn Oliver. St. Louis City Police Officer's wife. Bill Oliver, the city cop, murdered her and then attempted to frame James Leroy Cochran.

Detective Tom Rangel, Intelligence Unit. Good cop, good partner. Circa 1979.

Patrolman William Oliver; burglar, thief, murderer.
Murdered his wife because he thought she was going to
inform on him pertaining to his off-duty crimes. Tried to
frame James Leroy Cochran (jimmy) for her murder.

Jimmy with his best friend for life, Norm London. Norm's 80th birthday party, Kemoll's Restaurant, downtown St. Louis.

*youthful **Jimmy** Cochran*

Former ninth district cop, Michael Paul. Naval Intelligence, CIA Agent.

Leon Strauss with his adopted son, Adam Strauss.

Notorious gangster and bank robber, Max ᴉbᴇrꜱ
(Big-Maxie) Greenberg. Adam Strauss
alleges Max is his great, great grandfather.

James "Fat" Woods; (left) notorious heroin dealer in St. Louis, in the visiting room of the Leavenworth Federal Penitentiary. Virgil Atkins is the other inmate to the left of Fat; he was Fat's right-hand-man in the heroin trade. Incarceration melted the fat off of Fat.

DAVID E. RICHARDSON

David Richardson, small time criminal trying to break into the big-leagues. Shot Dead with a 12-gauge shotgun by Detective Frank Burns, Detective Robert Scheetz, Al Tucci., late 1950s.

THE DIVISION OF HEALTH OF MISSOURI
STANDARD CERTIFICATE OF DEATH

59-015602
STATE FILE NUMBER
Regist. 2-2840

MAY 1 1959 Registration District No. _____ Primary Registration District No. _____

CE OF DEATH ----
OUNTY

2. USUAL RESIDENCE (Where deceased lived. If institution: Residence before admission)
a. STATE Missouri   b. COUNTY

ITY (if outside corporate limits, give TOWNSHIP only)   Inside Limits Yes ☒ No ☐
OR OWN St. Louis

c. CITY OR TOWN St.Louis   Inside Limits Yes ☐ No ☐

ULL NAME OF (if NOT in hospital, give location)   Length of stay in institution
OSPITAL OR E/R To City Hosp. 21 Yrs.
STITUTION

d. STREET ADDRESS 1525 Missouri Ave.   Reside on Farm Yes ☐ No ☒

E OF DECEASED
a. or print)   First DAVID   Middle EUGENE   Last RICHARDSON

4. DATE OF DEATH   Month March   Day 18   Year 1959

6. COLOR OR RACE White   le ☐
7. MARRIED ☐ NEVER MARRIED ☒   WIDOWED ☐ DIVORCED ☐

8. DATE OF BIRTH 12-8-1936

9. AGE (In years) 22   IF UNDER 1 YEAR Months / Days   IF UNDER 24 HRS. Hours / Min.

AL OCCUPATION (Give kind of work done)   10b. KIND OF BUSINESS OR INDUSTRY
borer   Unemployed

11. BIRTHPLACE (City and state or country) Corydon, Ky.

12. CITIZEN OF WHAT COUNTRY? U.S.A.

ER'S NAME
lliam Richardson   13b. MOTHER'S MAIDEN NAME Zadie West   14. NAME OF HUSBAND OR WIFE Judith

DECEASED EVER IN U.S. ARMED FORCES? If yes, give war or dates of service
14. SOCIAL SECURITY NO.   17. INFORMANT William Richardson, Address 1525 Missouri Ave.

CAUSE OF DEATH (Enter only one cause per line for (a), (b), and (c).)
PART I. DEATH WAS CAUSED BY:
IMMEDIATE CAUSE (a) Internal hemorrhage following
Multiple gunshots of the chest and
Conditions, if any, which gave rise to the above causes (a), stating the underlying cause last.
DUE TO (b) abdomen   E984X
DUE TO (c) suffered ...

INTERVAL BETWEEN ONSET AND DEATH

PART II. OTHER SIGNIFICANT CONDITIONS ... in hands of police officer if official

WAS AUTOPSY PERFORMED? YES ☒ NO ☐

... police duty in area, in the vicinity of city jail, about 7:55 pm

HOMICIDE ☐

TIME OF INJURY 7:55 p.m.   Month, Day, Year March 18, 1959

INJURY OCCURRED
LE AT ☐ NOT WHILE ☐   AT WORK ☐
20b. PLACE OF INJURY (e.g. in or about home, farm, factory, office bldg., etc.) area, City Jail
20c. CITY, TOWN, OR LOCATION   COUNTY St. Louis   STATE Mo.

I attended the deceased from ... and last saw him alive on ... on the date stated above; and to the best of my knowledge, from the causes stated.
Death occurred at ...

IGNATURE ... (Degree or title)   22b. ADDRESS 1300 Clark   22c. DATE SIGNED 3-20-59

RIAL, CREMATION, 23a. DATE 3/21/1959   23b. NAME OF CEMETERY OR CREMATORY St.Trinity Lutheran   23c. LOCATION (City, town, or county) St.Louis County, Mo.
oval

ERAL DIRECTOR ... AUGHLIN'S, 2301 Lafayette Ave   25. DATE REC'D BY LOCAL REG. MAR 20 59   26. REGISTRAR'S SIGNATURE Earl Smith, M.D.

(Licensed Embalmer's Statement on Reverse Side)

David Eugene Richardson' death certificate.

The gang that couldn't shoot straight. Good idea for a crime, poor execution. They never let you down.

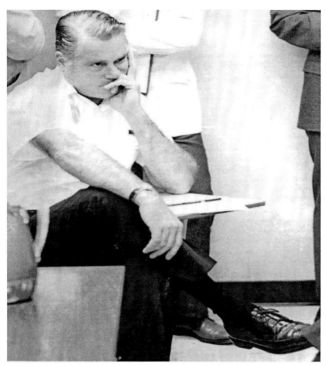

Legendary cop leader, Captain Harry Lee. Deep thinker; intelligent man.

Chief of Detectives, Lieutenant Colonel John Doherty. Every cop strived to be like him; He was a hero, a smooth guy, belonged to an exclusive country club, hobnobbed with the elite of the region. He killed the bad guy, and if you worked for him, chances are you followed his lead.

Hero cop Captain George Hollocher. Maligned by Internal Affairs and forced to retire.

Lombardo's Restaurant in its heyday, 1960's, 70's and 80's. Walnut Park changed drastically and they were forced out of the neighborhood. Lombardo's was the best of the best at that location, and still is across from Union Station at the Drury, Lombardo's Trattoria, owned and operated by Tony Lombardo.

Lombardo's Restaurant, Riverview and W. Florissant, the focal point of the once prestige Walnut Park neighborhood. Now sitting vacant.

10

   More irony, my friends: While Jimmy Cochran was languishing in prison, and befriending organized St. Louis criminals, crooks who came and went in the federal judicial system, leaving "prove a point" Jimmy snoozing in joint-land, this cop/writer was a detective in the Intelligence Unit, spying on his released prison friends. Guys like Ray Flynn, head of Laborers Local # 42, (lived with his mother on Faust Court in Oakville) who took his orders from Art Bernie, scummy eastside gangster who took his orders from Joey Aiuppa, head of the Outfit in Chicago. Ray placed a car bomb in John Paul Spica's car, and blew him to smithereens.

   Ray was the consummate jewel thief. He was like a wild animal when it came to home burglaries. He would force his way in and frantically ransack the house looking for a safe. Even if there was a burglar alarm he would try to break in and search before the cops could answer the alarm sounding. Ray walked with a limp, allegedly tortured by some cops who caught him burglarizing a home in Ladue. He had apparently broken his leg while trying to elude the cops, and they stood on his broken leg while he was down.

   One of the reasons Ray Flynn was such an aggressive burglar (besides the obvious money made from loose stones) was the fact that he had a fence for the diamonds he stole, and loose stones were prevalent with wealthy people.

   Jerry Chotin, of Kaiwin-Chotin Jewelers, in the Arcade Building in downtown St. Louis, fenced all of Ray Flynn's stones, no questions asked, and he paid Ray a fair price for the diamonds. Having an active fence in your pocket in the diamond theft business is a big plus.

   It made Ray Flynn a monster who would do anything to obtain more diamonds; it made Jerry Chotin wealthier than the other crooked diamond merchants in the St. Louis diamond trade. Buy super low, sell super high; the diamond merchant's creed.

Jerry Chotin brought his son, Ricky Chotin into the business. The goal was to make money, lots of it. Ricky Chotin devised a plan to purchase fractured diamonds and to fill them with a foreign substance, and sell them as perfect stones. Business was great for them, until another jeweler doing an insurance appraisal noticed that the stone was fractured and filled. An inquiry found that hundreds of fractured stones were sold by the Chotins.

Kawin-Chotin was sued by banks, insurance funds, and other jewelers, all of whom were as crooked as the Chotins, but they didn't get caught filling fractured stones; they just purchased stolen stones from professional gangsters, union executives, murderers and thieves, and resold them.

Arsenic is a standard cleaner for diamonds; it is prevalent in shops that work on and with diamonds. Ricky Chotin was feeling the pressure of his great idea imploding before his, and his dad's eyes; he drank some arsenic in their shop at the Paul Brown Building in downtown St. Louis (Paul Brown Building was the mecca for fencing or purchasing stolen diamonds). Ricky Chotin died in the shop. The beat goes on in the diamond trade. Jewelers still deal in stolen stones; it is why people are in the diamond trade.

Ray Flynn died in prison. Jimmy Cochran was out at the time, and he attended his funeral. Quite certain this cop detective/writer was there in the Intelligence Unit surveillance van taking photos of all who attended.

The bombing death of John Paul Spica, was the turning point for Ray Flynn. The feds targeted him, and Jesse Stoneking (super criminal, super snitch) got him on a wire bragging about a stolen refrigerator Ray had purchased. It's a felony in Missouri to purchase a stolen appliance.

Ray went down hard for a stupid offense. Greed got to him. There are very few smart crooks. Donald Ray Woolbright (did the Howard Hughes burglary in Los Angeles and got away with it) was famous for being cunning. His dad trained him to be the consummate crook.

Donnie Ray Woolbright was given a cache of diamonds to "hold on to" for diamond thief, Bosco Owens, while Bosco was vacationing in the federal penitentiary. Bosco got out and told Donnie Ray he was ready to take possession of his diamonds.

Of course, Donnie Ray had sold them and spent the money, probably before the van carrying federal prisoners arrived at the penitentiary. Donnie Ray was told to bring the stones to Bosco's house in St. Charles County. Donnie Ray took his brother with him. They murdered Bosco, shot him in the back of the head while he was urinating in his bathroom.

They put Bosco's body in the trunk of his own car, burned the house to the ground, and parked Bosco's car at Lambert Field (airport). It was below freezing, and Bosco's frozen corpse wasn't discovered for a couple of months. No one was ever arrested for Bosco Owens' murder. Donnie Ray Woolbright is now deceased.

Jimmy Cochran was incarcerated with Forest Parker at the Missouri State Penitentiary. Parker was one of Marvin Dale Berry's sidekicks. Burglar, stick-up man.

Billy Politte: associate of Jimmy's, burglar, stick-up man, murderer. Business agent for hoisting engineers 513. Lived near the canal in Granite City off of I-270. His brother, Jerry Politte was also a burglar, stick-up man, murderer.

Fred "Fritz" Wolfe: burglar, murderer, auto thief, head of Laborer Local 110. He was typical of union leadership in the St. Louis region. Jimmy was a close friend of his; he even purchased Fritz's 2003 Lincoln Continental Town Car Cartier from him. The union paid for it for Fritz. Jimmy got a deal on it.

And, to add insult to injury, Fred Wolfe was voted in (to run local # 110) by the majority of the laborers. He took Mike Trupiano's spot. Trupiano was the head of the St. Louis branch of the Chicago Mafia; even though he came from Detroit. He answered to Joey Aiuppa, in Chicago.

Jimmy knew Edward "Ted" Wortman: Brother of Frank "Buster" Wortman. Ted was a burglar, or anything else his brother wanted him to be. Frank was the head of organized crime in East St. Louis, Illinois for forty years. He took his orders from The Outfit in Chicago. Both were the scum of the earth.

Jimmy was associated with Art Berne, a burglar, and anything else crooked he could be. He took over organized crime on the eastside after Buster Wortman died. If there was anyone scummier than Buster Wortman, it was Art Berne.

We (Intelligence Unit detectives) knew most of these guys. On any given day, the two-man detective crews in the Intelligence Unit would come across these guys, sometimes randomly. Guys like Billy Politte, (living remotely in Granite City) were difficult to place under surveillance. We had a van with a periscope on top; we'd sit in a comfortable leather chair, kind of like a bucket seat in a sports car. It would revolve when we needed it to. We couldn't use the surveillance van at Billy Politte's compound.

The periscope had a .35 mm camera attached to it, and we could take as many photos as we wished. But the trick was, finding a place to park the van while we were surveilling. We covered all the gangster funerals and wakes. People would bang on the sides of the van and shout, "Have you no respect for the dead?"

We covered the airport, standing around with our hands in our pockets, or acting like we were reading a newspaper; watching for flights from New York, Los Angeles, Chicago, Las Vegas, watching for organized criminals to slide into St. Louis for a meeting with Sorkis Webbe Sr., or the dozens of international crooks who lived here. Jimmy knew them on the inside. The Intelligence Unit crews knew them on the outside.

Jimmy notes that he was indebted to several people in his life of crime, and during his rehabilitation from crook to "straight guy". He mentions his wife, and pastor, and a name I wasn't familiar with, John Paul Chase.

An inquiry informed me that John Paul Chase was a depression-era bank robber and outlaw. He was a longtime criminal associate of the Karpis-Barker Gang, and was a robber with Baby Face Nelson, who later brought him into the John Dillinger Gang. Jimmy was asked about his relationship with John Paul Chase.

Jimmy advised that during his second visit at Leavenworth, he was having trouble adjusting to prison life, and that he recognized a guy who had "snitched" on him while being detained at the St. Louis City Jail. Jimmy was planning an escape from the city jail; Seems like everyone was.

These guys in lock-up, don't realize that their demeanor and their "snitching" stay with them for eternity. People hate "snitches"; cops hate them, relatives hate them, the people who they "snitch" on hate them enough to kill them. They're kind of like barn burners in rural communities. They're hated but feared. No one has any defense against a barn burner, except to kill them.

Jimmy was assigned to "A" block in the prison, "A" block was the most un-livable cell block to be in, cells were crowded, and the populace was insane. "A" block was loud, with people screaming and yelling, and fighting. "D" block was where the old timers were housed. People spoke in hushed tones there, and there was one man to a cell. "A" block was getting to Jimmy Cochran.

Jimmy and a group of convicts were marching to the mess hall, going up a set of steel stairs in a crook line; the "snitch" knew that Jimmy had it in for him, and it was a situation wherein the convict who strikes first was going to be the winner; survival of the fittest; Jimmy stabbed the "snitch" in the back, twice with his home-made prison shiv; never turn your back on your enemy.

The "snitch" lived, but Jimmy was thrown in the "hole" for ten-days, and was isolated for twelve months. He wanted out of isolation, but he also wanted out of "A" block. It was driving him nuttier than he already was. He did his detention in the hole and returned to "A" block.

It should be noted: the inmates control the prison. The guards are there to just keep the peace, kind of like St. Louis cops who patrol the African American villages of north St. Louis. The convict in charge of Leavenworth was John Paul Chase. He lived in "D" block, and if anything went down within the prison walls, he was apprised of it. He knew Jimmy Cochran, and he was at times kind to him.

When the Federal Bureau of Prisons bureaucrats visited Leavenworth, they had a meeting with John Paul Chase. They wanted to appease him, for keeping the peace within the walls of a federal prison is largely the responsibility of the convict in charge of the institution.

Jimmy set up a meeting with John Paul Chase. He asked him to get him transferred to "D" block. It was the difference between heaven and hell. John Paul Chase honored Jimmy's request.

11

There were three factions of organized crime in the St. Louis region in the 50s, 60s, 70s, and 80s: The eastside faction, the Italian Mafia, and the Syrian faction. All the aforementioned criminals were beholden, in one way or another, to one or more of these crime factions. Jimmy Cochran was associated with members of these groups.

All the factions were indirectly controlled by the Chicago Mafia. As the heads of the Chicago Mafia died, were killed, or were sent to prison, a new "boss" would be appointed. Those days, in Chicago, there were three bosses: Tony Accardo, Joey Aiuppa, and Gus Alex.

The eastside faction, once controlled by Frank "Buster" Wortman, and Art Berne after Buster Wortman died, was just a branch office of the Chicago Outfit. Art Berne and his killers, burglars, arsonists, bomb makers, and union executives, answered to Joey Aiuppa.

But an amazing revelation came to pass. Joe Cammarata, an underboss of the St. Louis Mafia faction, and a member of Pipefitters Local # 562, the wealthiest trade union in the United States of America, was elected to the executive board of the union.

He was loyal to Joey Aiuppa, Art Berne, and any member of the Chicago, or eastside faction. The Chicago Outfit, now had control of Pipefitters, Local # 562 through eastside scum dog, Art Berne, and controlled it for decades.

The Italian faction in St. Louis was loosely controlled by Matthew "Mike" Trupiano. He also was the President of Laborers local # 110. Joey Aiuppa was his boss, but since he was a "made guy", and was actually a member of the Detroit Mafia family. Joey Aiuppa was calling the shots concerning Mike Trupiano, and laborers local #110.

With Ray Flynn being in control of labor local # 42, with his loyalty to Art Berne, and Joey Aiuppa, Chicago had organized labor just about sewed up in the St. Louis region, including the Teamsters. Nino Parrino was a "made guy" within the Mafia, just like his bosom buddy, Joe Cammarata of Pipefitters Local # 562 The Department of Justice, broke up that party when they took control of the Teamsters Union.

 Nino Parrino was a principal in Teamsters local # 682 and was reputedly also an underboss of the St. Louis Mafia. Nino was forced out of the Teamsters, and so was his boss and mentor, Bobby Sansone. Bobby Sansone was a politician who would play any side to get ahead.

Joe Cammarata hired Nino as a Pipefitter, and gave him a Pipefitters # 562 membership card. Nino never set foot on a job site, but was paid handsomely, with pension benefits, for doing absolutely nothing.

Guys like Detectives George Venegoni, Tim Reagan, and this cop/writer, assisted by FBI Agent Tom Fox, tried to keep tabs on all the organized crime guys in the region. We were always on the outside looking in, and we had to surmise what was going on.

Someone in the Intelligence Unit needed to interview Nino Parrino. Not because we might learn something we didn't already know, but just to let the organized creep/crooks know we are watching them, and despise them.

 An idea was concocted for a unit detective to go inside of Nino's office and interview him, all we were doing was harassing these crime brokers. Hardly any cases were made on them. It was apparent some cop/detective needed to yank Nino's chain and see what happens.

The cop/writer waltzed into Teamsters Headquarters, 300 South Grand (near St. Louis University), told the receptionist he needed to talk to Nino Parrino, and was asked what his business was.

Cheapo business cards were available to us so one was slid onto this cute receptionist' desk. She was too attractive to be a mob moll, and it was apparent she was related to someone within the union. These guys only trust relatives. She walked away, into the inner sanctum of Teamster organized crime; fancy office, big desks, views from the windows; sexy secretaries.

Eventually she escorted cop/writer into Nino's palatial office. He was a thug, and he did everything he could to play the role. Problem he had was that he was not a physical guy. He was a puke, dressed in an expensive suit; the guy who gives the orders for someone who is physical, to assault, or maim, or kill someone who Nino is at odds with.

The cop/writer's dislike for him was difficult to hide. In a perfect world, Nino would have been snatched from behind his desk and pummeled with eastside, Marine Corps fists.

The assault could've been accomplished and gotten away with. St. Louis cop Detectives, particularly in Intelligence, could do no wrong; we worked at the discretion of the Chief of Police; we were his special unit.

The detective could, and would say he was defending himself. Nino Parrino was a gangster, a Chicago led Mafioso. The cop brain analyzed what Nino was; he was the same as the bosses in the police department. Pukes with power; ordering someone else to do their dirty work.

Nino was Lieutenant Phil Pizzo, with a shiny Italian suit, and diamond rings. Except for John Doherty, this young detective had a tough time mustering up a respect for any of them. John Doherty had proven himself; he was a legend.

So, with this cop's hatred of Nino Parrino slightly diminishing, the question was finally posed; "How is it that a "made Mafia guy" like you, can have a big-time Teamster job, sitting behind a desk and acting important?"

Nino came unhinged. He tried to intimidate writer/cop by shouting, "What?" he screamed. "Who told you that?"

Nino was constantly being measured, and it appeared he had reached the point in the character assassination of him that he would rise-up behind his desk and become a physical threat.

Intelligence Unit Detectives feel important, driven, dedicated, but in reality, we are wise-assed-cop-detectives who enjoy disrespecting rich and powerful gangsters in their plush union offices. Nino was the criminal creep of the Teamster Mafia. It was his turf.

There was an instant plan; if he physically threatens, or makes aggressive or threatening moves, Nino will get his ass kicked; Just an old-fashioned ass kicking; fists and feet, and maybe an occasional knee to the balls.

But the Mafia prick, puke, didn't stand, not even behind the safety of his desk. He just shouted and wanted to know who the cop/writer worked for, and typical Teamster, organized labor/crime bullshit that puke assholes like him shout on a daily basis.

People ran into his office; standing and facing them, they stood out in the sunlight coming in from the large windows; they were also puke's with suits; quite certain Bobby Sansone was one of them. They didn't get near, not within striking distance. They stared, like the cop/writer had just insulted the Pope inside of the Vatican; there was disbelief in their eyes.

It was time to back out of the office; this was a crucial time in the programmed insult/assault of the St. Louis Mafia. Doorways are always dangerous; puke gangsters pay underlings to assault naysayers at portals of ingress and egress. The Teamster office was a cesspool of crime.

Parking lots are super dangerous if an assailant wants to do bodily harm. The unit/staff detective car was a safe haven; the department legal .38 was in-hand; no one followed. The tape was played for Venegoni and Reagan, and all shared a laugh.

If John Doherty, Chief of Detectives would have walked into Nino's office, instead of Detective Tim Richards, Nino Parrino, underboss of the St. Louis Mafia scene, would not have put on a show, shouting and cursing and acting tough. He would have stacked cash on his desk; begged for leniency; blamed his Mafia existence on someone else.

It is unknown who dreamed up the police department plan on how to silently motivate police officers to go above and beyond the call of duty, but whoever, he/she was, was a genius. The mere presence of John Doherty struck fear in the hearts and minds of career criminals. The presence of Detective Tim Richards caused dismay.

Maybe part of John Doherty's legacy was myth, it doesn't matter. He was a figurehead for cops to overextend themselves. He was a cop god, and he was revered for decades within, and outside of the police department.

The third crime family was the Syrian Faction; it wasn't comprised of Syrians; it was Lebanese, and how the two countries came about in reference to organized crime in St. Louis, Missouri is a mystery.

But the Lebanese were immigrants who settled here in old St. Louis. They were different than the Muslim mid-eastern tribes; they were Maronite Christians and belonged to St. Raymond's Catholic Church in the French Quarter of St. Louis, (Soulard).

In most part, they were hard working businessmen, and politicians. Many of them worked to get college degrees, some were lawyers. The head of the Syrian faction was Sorkis Webbe Sr. He was a lawyer, businessman (owned the Mayfair Hotel in downtown St. Louis) and owned The Aladdin Hotel and Casino in Las Vegas.

The Leisure family, Lebanese, businessmen and labor people, were silently involved with organized crime in and around St. Louis. Paul Leisure (John Paul Leisure) was a killer for hire and was used by anyone with the cash to pay him.

Joey Aiuppa allegedly used Paul Leisure occasionally to make vocal opponents disappear. Paul Leisure was an insane monster. He wasn't like Nino Parrino or any of the Italian faction Mafioso; Paul was a physical monster; scary to look at or converse with.

Doubtful if any Intelligence Unit Detectives, or any FBI agents would ever approach Paul Leisure for a chat. It would be insanity to enter Paul Leisure's domain for an interview. Good possibility the interviewer would never be seen again.

Paul's brother, Anthony Leisure is still alive, incarcerated for life in the Missouri State Penitentiary for murder. He was a smooth, pimp sort of fellow, but he was an aggressive traveling burglar, specializing in home invasions of wealthy, questionable men who he had done business with. He was a diamond thief and a burglar.

One of the guys Anthony Leisure traveled and invaded with was George Eidson. They were the gruesome twosome. George Eidson is now a wealthy man of leisure. Word travels quickly in the diamond/burglar circuit. Large stones, big scores, out of town buyers of loose stones, this information is collected by the burglars, and plans are made to get into the houses of the wealthy who purchase the loose diamonds.

The diamonds can't be identified outside of the settings, brooches, or necklaces. It's something the thief can place in his pocket, after the setting is destroyed. It isn't against the law to have a cache of loose diamonds in your possession. They aren't controlled substances, or weapons. They are owned by the person who has them in their possession.

The criminal Leisures, (Paul and Anthony) wanted to control labors local # 110. That local controlled labor jobs south of Chouteau Avenue in the City of St. Louis, and St. Louis County. Joey Aiuppa (Chicago Outfit) had some control of local # 110 through old gangster Jimmy Michaels. Michaels once worked for Buster Wortman in East St. Louis, Illinois. He was a killer, pimp, burglar; anything Buster desired of him. Jimmy Michaels association with the Chicago Outfit was old, but strong.

The Leisures, especially Paul Leisure, hated Jimmy Michaels. Jimmy was being protected by Anthony Giordano, one of the capos of Chicago Organized crime in St. Louis. Paul Leisure advised Tony Giordano that he was going to kill Jimmy Michaels and take over the criminal faction of labor local # 110. Tony Giordano told him to leave Jimmy Michaels alone or there would be hell to pay.

Tony Giordano died of natural causes on August 29, 1980, his wake and funeral were attended by Intelligence Unit detectives; our surveillance van was parked across from the funeral home.

The Leisures, led by Madman Paul Leisure, had been waiting for this moment. Jimmy Michaels was a celebrity in the little burg of St. Louis. He had gotten people jobs, kissed babies, and shaken hands since he relocated to the Missouri side of the Mississippi River and turned his back on the eastside and turned his attention to union corruption, and laborers local # 110.

Jimmy Michaels cruised around town in a yellow Chrysler Cordoba, and ate lunch at St. Raymond's Maronite Catholic

Church every Wednesday. It was where most of the organized criminal union officials met and dined.

Paul Leisure, his brother Anthony, and cousin, David Leisure, practiced making car bombs but never could succeed. They purchased a Chrysler Cordoba and practiced attaching a makeshift bomb to the undercarriage of the car. They had it down pat, but they were unsure about their bomb making expertise, so they asked a business associate, Fred Prather, to make it for them.

Bomb making, especially remote-control detonating car bombs, was a skill most of the eastside burglars were capable of doing. It was so easy to commission someone to make a bomb for a customer; it was like ordering a delivered pizza. Fred Prather did a good job; he was a smart guy, and ruthless, just like the Leisure's. Problem was Fred had a conscience.

So, Wednesday, September 17, 1980 rolled around and Anthony Leisure and his retarded cousin, David Leisure, drove onto the lot at St. Raymond's. David crawled under the Cordoba and sat the bomb on top of the transmission. It took him thirty seconds, investigators estimated. David climbed back into the car with Anthony Leisure, and they drove off St. Raymond's lot and waited for Jimmy Michaels to come out and drive away.

September and October are totally gorgeous in old St. Louis, and this particular day the weather was superb, about eighty degrees, light breeze, trees full, grass green, birds were singing, and Jimmy Michaels was content. His belly was full of Lebanese food, he was wealthy, elderly, (75) had a lot of children and grandchildren, and people, in general, respected him. Isn't that pretty much what we all strive for in life?

Jimmy headed south on I-55, with Anthony, and David Leisure, a fair distance behind him. Anthony was driving, and he gave his retarded cousin the order to ignite the bomb.

David always followed Anthony's orders. He would carry out any order given to him by Paul or Anthony.

The bomb blew the Cordoba to pieces; the entire car flew up into the air about five feet, and then came down with a thud on the shoulder. Jimmy's lower body was gone. It looked like he had been surgically dismembered form his upper torso. Dynamite is a bitch!

The mob war began; all for control of those stupid labor unions. Jimmy's relatives were placed in protective custody by the federal government. Word leaked out of the Leisure faction that Madman Paul Leisure wanted to kill every Michaels, grandchildren included. Federal agents came into the parochial schools and retrieved the Michaels children, during classes. It was the talk of the southside. People were concerned and afraid.

A grandchild, and a nephew of Jimmy Michaels, all with good jobs within organized labor in the region, decided they would get revenge with the Leisures. They enlisted help from the Chief of Police of St. George, a small municipality in south St. Louis County, Russ Schepp. The Michaels were spoiled offspring of a gangster. Russ Schepp owed Jimmy Michaels and the Michaels family for past favors. They were amateurs, being lured into a game of death by a master killer.

By this time, October 15, 1982, Paul Leisure was a business agent for the other mob-controlled labor union, local # 42. It was being controlled by Ray Flynn, burglar, gangster, murderer, a tough guy who also lived with his mother; the union is now being run by his nephew, Brandon Flinn, (purposely spells his name with an I instead of a y) who's dad Malcolm Flynn was a bomb maker for hire.

Russ Schepp, and James Michaels III, grandson of gangster Jimmy Michaels, made the bomb that blew up Paul Leisure for retaliation of the bombing of Jimmy Michaels. They placed the bomb under the Cadillac of Paul Leisure, positioned under the driver's seat, sitting on the brick roadway.

They waited in an alley across the street from Paul Leisure's mom's house (Paul lived with his mother) on Bischof at Kingshighway. Paul had a remote starter on his Cadillac, and he started the car and came out to climb in. He was wearing his blue laborer's helmet with PAUL LEISURE, BUSINESS AGENT, emblazoned on it.

Russ Schepp, and jimmy Michaels III, watched, but they watched too long. Paul placed the Cadillac in reverse and was able to back up before Russ Schepp or Jimmy Michaels III detonated the bomb. They had buck fever, and they had played their hand. The FBI and the ATF and the local cops in the bombing and arson unit jumped on the Michaels kid, and Russ Schepp.

The feds eventually found out that Jimmy Michaels III had rented an apartment in the little Jefferson County, Missouri burg of Arnold. They searched the apartment, which was filled with bombmaking material, and an instructional, and found bomb making items in the dumpster outside. They were amateurs trying to act like pros.

Both Schepp, and Michaels III had lived with the stories of revenge, and organized crime, and union control for most of their lives, but when it comes time to orchestrate and perform murder, things get cloudy for the amateur. Schepp, and Michaels III were arrested. They hired Norm London as their defense lawyer.

There were flashbacks of the bloody ninth district, Glen Vaughn, Phil Pizzo, Jimmy Cochran, and Norm London. Norm London was a fixture in the CWE. One of his wives had a boutique in the 4600 block of McPherson. She lived above it. Norm would be seen occasionally visiting her shop. He was known on sight by many ninth district cops. Norm would notice a cop cruising by on patrol, but he would not acknowledge. He didn't know any beat cops, but he probably knew John Doherty.

The bomb didn't kill Paul Leisure. It tore him up, but the impact of the dynamite was weakened by the cowl of the Cadillac. But Paul was out of the picture. It was his last hurrah, except showing off in court while sitting in a wheelchair.

Anthony and David Leisure continued their bombing campaign. They blew up a cousin of Jimmy Michaels, Sonny Faheen, in a parking garage in the Mansion House Apartments in downtown St. Louis. Then they shot to death an associate, Michael Kornhardt, in a field in St. Charles County, near the Mississippi River.

Fred Prather, genius mechanic and bomb maker, came to the FBI and cooperated; Fred ad previously advised Paul Leisure that if any harm came to Michael Kornhardt, he was going to walk out on Paul. Other killers in the Leisure gang wanted to do the same, but the FBI didn't need them, they had Fred Prather. The entire gang was arrested and held without bail. Those who could, made a plea agreement with the feds.

Paul Leisure and his brother Anthony, and their retarded cousin David Leisure, went to court, and lost. Paul died in the federal prison hospital in Springfield, Missouri. Anthony is still incarcerated in the state penitentiary in Farmington, Missouri. He'll never get out. David Leisure was executed.

This labor movement corruption, murder, car bombings, diamond burglaries, and Chicago Outfit control over St. Louis politics, all the way to the state capitol, was for naught. The party was about to end.

FBI Agent, Tom Fox, enlisted Jesse Stoneking to turn into a snitch for him and the federal government. Tom interviewed Jesse in the federal penitentiary in Marion, Illinois. Jesse was upset because Art Berne promised him that the he and the organization would care for Jesse's two complete families for him while he was incarcerated.

Art Berne lied. No honor among thieves. So, Jesse was primed for revenge against everyone involved with, or somehow attached to crime in St. Louis, eastside, and anywhere else in the region. Everyone involved knew Jesse, and they loved to brag to him about their criminal endeavors. Jesse was wired, and he got them all. Organized crime, Chicago style, was gone, and it has never returned. (Crooks Kill, Cops Lie. Cop/writer's nonfiction book).

Dope smuggling was now the way for criminal entrepreneurs to beat the system. Much more lucrative than union corruption; less risk, and the Colombians were giving the weed on consignment.

Jimmy Cochran style bank robbing? Old time, high percentage of failure, and damned dangerous. Jimmy was once asked if he ever got away with any bank robberies; it was difficult to imagine continuing with the same crime and never being successful at it. He said, "Yes!"

12

It was time to look for a new home within the St. Louis Metropolitan Police Department. It was 1984, Orwellian in every way. New supervisors were amongst us; us being the guys and gals who did the work within the unit. They tapped our office telephones, and at times our home telephones. How could George Orwell have had such insight?

The organized crime game in the St. Louis region was gone, thanks to Jesse Stoneking. The guys and gals in the unit who actually worked the organized criminals didn't know whether to love Jesse or hate him, but it was obvious the good gig in Intelligence was coming to a close.

This unit detective threatened to kill Jesse one day on a car stop; he was wired by the FBI; obviously no one had access to that fact, except the FBI and Jesse. Jesse had just met with Mike Trupiano, the reputed head of the Italian Mafia faction, taping their conversation for future incarceration for Mike.

So, a crazed cop threatened to kill a mobster; small problem of explanation for the cop; it could be written out of. Jesse was the king of snitches, something law enforcement can't do without, but as a person, we despise snitches. The rule of thumb: all criminals are snitches; except James Leroy Cochran.

We (unit detectives) despised the organized crooks as we spied upon them; Nino Parrino, Art Berne, Mike Trupiano; We despised them all. But in the true nature of this detective, being born in East St. Louis, Illinois, the Intelligence Unit bosses were held in the same esteem.

The working Intelligence Unit detectives were hearing rumbles of information concerning the remaining few professional criminals in the trade and labor unions; they were switching to drug smuggling. Weed, (marijuana) had always been the drug of choice in most communities. These union aficionados knew about dope, and how to get it on consignment for resale.

There were other drugs attached to the smuggling of weed. Quaaludes, a psychotic drug used by someone who completely desires to tone out on the reality of life, and cocaine, an opiate that eventually took America over. Dopers use it when they can't get marijuana.

Just being a weed smuggler had romantic vibes to it: boats, airplanes, exotic cars, beautiful women, palm trees and beaches. What more could a professional criminal ask for? The Colombians had different plans for Americano's; If you got 1000 pounds of weed, you also had to take a certain percentage of Quaaludes, and cocaine.

There was no discussion with the Colombians. Business in the drug trade was dependent upon them. There was always someone willing to do their duty, so the amateur, wealthy drug heroes of the land of opportunity, sold hard drugs, along with the weed.

There was an abundance of amateur weed smugglers in the area; a couple of wealthy kids from St. Clair County, Illinois, whose parents owned successful restaurants in Belleville, Illinois, had pilot's licenses', and airplanes. They would fly to south Florida and bring back loads of weed. They were wealthy to begin with, and they got wealthier. If a guy had cojones, or a little cash, he could be rich in a couple of years. Miami Beach was built on illegal dope cash, and probably most of the state of Florida. And the dope barons got away with it.

One of the Teamster Locals, # 600, was filled with criminals, just like Labor Local # 42. The word was drifting into Intelligence that Rick Yackey, a north St. Louis County guy, (a guy mentioned earlier) was supplying (on consignment) cocaine to a guy in local # 600, Paul Wayne King, who went by a shortened version of his name, Wayne King.

Wayne King was and is a tough guy. Rick Yackey was driven by greed from childhood. He joined the Paul Robinson smuggling group at a young age; started out as a courier, and then was the guy who ran the operation. He was able to communicate with the Colombians on their level. Paul Robinson would devastate the cash the group made. He was a money spending monster.

Paul wouldn't spend money on things like cars, or houses, or boats; he rented a house in Hollywood, Florida. He took taxis; if the group needed a boat, he paid someone to steal one for him. Paul wasted money on cocaine for personal usage, and on two ex-wives and their cocaine usage. Paul went through $100,000 a month on dope and women.

The group was getting dope consigned from Colombians, through a broker in south Florida. Rick Yackey quickly became friends with the broker; it didn't take long for the Colombians to realize Paul Robinson was not a guy to be in business with. He was an eastside thug who didn't pay his tab and he had three brothers who were also eastside thugs: Rich, Ervin, and Dan.

At the height of their drug-smuggling-venture they were all super rich. Paul was the extreme boss; if a member didn't like the way the business was being run, he'd kill them. The St. Louis Mafia leader, Mike Trupiano, went to Paul Robinson and advised him that he wanted a cut of the Robinson group's dope business, since the drugs were being sold and consigned in the St. Louis region. Paul Robinson told Trupiano to "fuck off" and Trupiano walked away with his tail between his legs.

Union office interviews were the forte in Intelligence; fish where the fish are. Build a rapport with the bosses. They were all crooked and paranoid, so they were extra friendly to unit cops. Wayne King resented my visits to the union offices and he let me know it. I told him to "fuck off" and he stayed away from me, but I knew what he was; badass, leg breaker for the union, and a dope dealer.

13

In the winter of 1986, after some heavy negotiations and some gigantic political favors, this confused, cop detective was transferred out of the Intelligence Unit and into the Drug Enforcement Administration (DEA) Task Force.

Why the confusion? The good and bad factor; having been indoctrinated from puberty not to lie, it was apparent that law enforcement was based on lying. The underling cop isn't pressured as much to lie while on patrol duty, but in the specialized units (where the cop detective is important) lying is a tool of the trade.

This cop/writer balked at lying; big mistake for the good approach. Hope springs eternal; lying isn't always required on the federal level. Hatred described the federal level experience at the beginning: being important was the trademark of the Intelligence Unit detective; being a worker, instead of a thinker, was the game plan now.

Rational men and women adjust or die. Being away from the St. Louis Metropolitan Police Department was like being on vacation. The Drug Enforcement Administration owned our asses; being a fed was cool.

We all had a company car (seized dope dealer car) and jeans and pull over Polo shirts, and expensive exotic cowboy boots, and federal DEA credentials; sworn in as a fed and sent to DEA fed school; got paid federal agent pay; worked with other cops and federal agents from around the region (St. Louis County and State Highway Patrol undercover cops).

There was access to a federal computer, and the daytime hours were slow in the Task Force. Our offices were in a bank building in Clayton, Missouri, the financial and political headquarters of the St. Louis region.

The curiosity of a cop detective focused on the federal computer: out of boredom, the names of criminals from the past, organized and union crooks, were crammed into the super-secret fed computer. It seemed like most crooks were now dope dealers.

James Leroy Cochran was a curiosity frequently; mainly because he was in the sights of a Remington Wingmaster shotgun a long time ago and the trigger wasn't squeezed; or maybe because bank robbing was an archaic way of making money. Jimmy was a criminal/convict, and convicts exchange ideas on how to make easy cash when they are eventually released. Dope smuggling and dealing was big talk in the incarceration world.

A Missouri Department of Corrections check on Jimmy Cochran revealed he was released from Leavenworth in 1984, and was in a halfway house in St. Louis, (St. Mary's,) on Papin down in the city near some projects. He was scheduled to be released from the halfway house in 1985, but was advised that he was given wrong information, and that he had to stay for an extra year.

Jimmy was released from St. Mary's halfway house in 1986. He got a job at Taco Bell on South Grand in the City of St. Louis, making tacos, mopping and sweeping. He wasn't there for long and he was hired as a salesman for Roach Equipment Company. The Roach Company sold shelving. Jimmy the bank robber was a salesman. Jimmy could be a congenial person when he wished to. His abductees even liked him; they didn't want to testify against him. He could con his bosses, if he liked them.

Jimmy was still in remission; would James Leroy Cochran snap again and rob banks, or smuggle dope, or deal drugs? Seeing him again in an official capacity would be awkward.

The status of Wayne King wasn't checked; unknown why, except that union halls and corruption was in the past. Although Wayne King is and was the kind of guy one wants to forget. He's like a caged animal in a zoo; dangerous but not to me.

The first dope deal was a buy-bust, meaning an undercover DEA agent, (task force guy) was making a hand-to-hand drug purchase from a stranger who had boasted about having access to loads of cocaine. Word spreads quickly in the dope business, just like the diamond and car bomb making business.

Joe Spiess, a St. Louis County narcotics detective, (now the Chief of Police of the Brentwood, Missouri Police Department) had set up a meeting, and a possible sale with a dealer Joe spoke with on the telephone.

Joe had gotten his name and telephone number from another drug dealer who had been arrested. They all turn their sources. Joe told the guy he had cash and wanted to purchase a couple of pounds of cocaine from the dope creature. Joe looked young; the DEA cops looked, and were young.

The deal went down, and the cocaine dealer was arrested, handcuffed, beaten in the back of a DEA surveillance van., and forced to identify his source for the dope. Badass Teamster, Wayne King was the source of the cocaine.

The group wasn't privy to this information; our information was that we as a small group, maybe six or seven cops and federal agents were going to have the arrested guy deliver the DEA cash, which had been photo copied, to the source at a hotel room in downtown St. Louis.

As a group, in separate cars, we converged on the swanky hotel, (where I once hobnobbed with politicos as part of my Intelligence Unit gig). The party was in the executive suite, which was soundproof. The arrested and beaten dope dealer who had sold the cocaine to Joe Spiess, had a key to the door; he unlocked it and the sound of hard rock blasted out at us. Someone pushed the dope dealer inside of the suite and we all followed him in.

It was huge party, maybe thirty stoned and drunk dope zombies. They stared at us as if we were going to rob them. We were shouting for everyone to get on the floor, or to get on the walls, or to turn the fucking stereo off.

Wayne King was standing near me. He was shoved and turned against the wall. The little .38 Smith & Wesson pistol was in my hand. Wayne tried to grab it. He was doped to the max, and he looked like a dead man walking.

The cops and robber's game is strange; cops deal with so many people they can't catalog all of them into their brains for instant identification; Wayne King recognized the former Intelligence Unit spy, now drug fed.

It was a terrible fight; the worst fight of this cop/Marine' life. Wayne King was admitted to the Springfield, Missouri Federal Prison Hospital in critical condition. He almost died. He lost a finger in the fight; no one knows how. None of us chomped it off, that is a fact. Wayne King was and is a badass.

After the fight in the hotel room, and after the spy/narc's face was covered in ice packs and he was nursed back to health, the realization of who Wayne King was came to light. The cocaine belonged to restauranteur, and hustler, Rick Yackey, of the Paul Robinson drug group. It was information privy to spy/cop from a year or so back, while a detective in Intelligence.

It all made sense after the brain returned to its normal size and the face swelling subsided. Rick Yackey, and Wayne King were both north St. Louis County guys. Wayne had access to the Teamster local # 600 guys, and lots of other lowlife thugs.

Cocaine had replaced weed in the get high for life crowd, mainly because weed had temporarily dried up: heroin, too.

Paul Robinson was languishing in a state penitentiary in Florida. The Hollywood, Florida Police Narcotics Unit did a search warrant on his rented house and Paul went away for a state paid vacation.

Rick Yackey, and Dan Robinson, the St. Louis marketing part of the gang, continued to sell cocaine in St. Louis. Rick got it on consignment from Colombian connections in Southeast Florida.

Dope smugglers and dealers don't want their dope; they want the cash the dope brings them, so they consign their product to whoever will take it, and market it. It's the most dangerous part of the dope game. Wayne King was a natural dope dealer; well known, tough badass, union man.

But the intelligence information on Rick Yackey, Wayne King, and any of the other partiers at the hotel suite was moot. It didn't matter. On the Task Force, it was kick in the door, seize anything of value, any contraband, arrest and incarcerate anyone in sight, and move onto the next target.

Wayne King went away for a federal vacation. He only did four or so years, got out and returned to Teamster Local # 600. The confused, spy/detective/narc resided near Wayne King, in north county and Spanish Lake, a federally targeted area for welfare blacks to take over. The county was huge, but our eyes locked often. We never acknowledged one another, not even a nod; neither of us looked down or sideways.

Rick Yackey, and Dan Robinson, were far from my mind. The guys and gals we took off in the Task Force were usually selling small quantities of dope; We, as a group, would try to take the dope up two or more notches to the source, but that only worked one time and then everyone in the dope groups knew someone had been taken off and snitched on the rest of them.

There were dope deals most every night. Small, quick deals, but time consuming on the part of the DEA cops and agents. There were arraignments, bond hearings, and meetings with Assistant United States Attorney's. And there were nights in bars with the groups of guys in federal law enforcement reinforcing the invisible bond between the different agencies, except the FBI. DEA Agents and the other groups hated the FBI. They were the bogeymen of federal law enforcement. Not much home time with the wife and kids. Glen Vaughn flashbacks were prevalent.

Paul Robinson was released from the Florida State Penitentiary; he returned to St. Louis with a vengeance. He demanded cash from Rick Yackey, and his brother Dan Robinson. In Paul Robinson's demented mind, the dope business being operated by Rick and Dan while he was incarcerated was still his. Any money they earned from it while he was gone was partially his.

If there was anyone scummier than Paul Robinson, it was his friend Tommy Venezia. Tommy owned a horse stable/riding stables ranch near Creve Coeur, (now a golf course). When Paul got released from prison, he went to Tommy Venezia seeking shelter. Tommy wouldn't allow Paul Robinson to enter his house, but Tommy had a camper/trailer on his property that was livable, so Paul and his wife Ellen resided in a camper on Venezia's ranch.

An informant revealed that the notorious Paul Robinson was living in a camper at Venezia's, so a rolling surveillance was in order. A rolling surveillance is where the cops roll by a location seeking information, being surreptitious.

The Intelligence Chevy detective car was steered out to Creve Coeur and the stables were checked out. There had been storms the area and Creve Coeur lake was over its banks and getting worse. Our car was making wakes as it was driven onto the Venezia property. We poked around, not caring if anyone observed us. Venezia and Robinson were vermin to us.

An attractive young woman came out of the Venezia house and advised to leave. "You are trespassing on private property and you had better leave. The owner is no one to mess with. He'll hurt you guys," she advised us.

It was obvious we were cops; our plain Jane Chevy and our appearance gave us up, we weren't trying to be undercover; we were just looking for an excuse to harass Tommy Venezia and Paul Robinson; we even went to the extent of looking into the camper through an uncovered window. Paul Robinson's big head and black eyes was there looking back at us. We drove away, into the flooding roads around the lake.

In St. Louis in the spring, if the Mississippi River doesn't get you, then the Missouri, or the Meramec, or the Big River, or the Gasconade, will. Tommy Venezia, several years later, murdered a young woman companion and then killed himself in Belleville, Illinois. From the photos in the Belleville, Illinois newspaper, the victim was the same attractive girl who warned us about him.

Paul Robinson, being a fair and honest guy had an offer for Rick Yackey, and his brother, Dan Robinson: "Give me a third of all proceeds earned in the last ten years, and I won't kill you and your children." That Paul, he's all heart! Rick had been ratholing money for his entire life. Money was god to him.

Dan splurged his income: he had girlfriends, a wife, children and he liked to big-time it in restaurants, and he hobnobbed with Norm London, and other reputable people. Dan had friends. He spent money on them and with them.

Rick and Dan ponied up some cash for Paul Robinson. He got an apartment in west St. Louis County with his most recent wife. She had been hustling (hair business) while Paul was on his ten-year Florida vacation. Paul was back in his old mode: live off of someone else. He never had a job in his life. He was a user and an abuser.

Rick Yackey decided to step the drug business up a notch to appease Paul Robinson. He had an employee who drove to Florida and picked up loads of cocaine. The guy rented cars at the airport in St. Louis, drove to Fort Lauderdale, loaded the bricks of cocaine into the trunk and drove back to St. Louis.

It was easy money, but Rick was overextending himself; greed was setting in since Paul came back on the scene. Paul was a ravaging animal when it came to money; no amount could satisfy him.

As in any game; sports, business, romance; over extension leads to mistakes. The word was out that Rick Yackey's courier was making frequent trips to Fort Lauderdale and bringing back loads of cocaine. Snitches are everywhere; anyone who ever worked federal law enforcement can vouch for that statement.

A new Special Agent came to the Task Force, Mike Braun. He was a hard charger and he was serious as a heart attack about success in DEA. He was number one in his DEA Academy class, which isn't an easy task, and he could have gone to any duty station in the world, but he chose St. Louis.

Mike Braun was all Marine, all cop, and all DEA Agent. On February 7, 1985, DEA Special Agent Enrique "Kiki" Camerana, was kidnapped, tortured, and murdered in Guadalajara, Mexico. Mike Braun was an investigator for the Illinois State Police. He had a wife and son who lived in neighboring Cape Girardeau, Missouri. Life was good for Mike.

Mike was traumatized by the murder of Kiki Camerana. He interviewed and tested for employment at DEA and was hired. Heroes are made not born. He went off to DEA and left his wife and child in Cape. They divorced. Mike was not only all DEA, he expected everyone around him to have his attitude; his often-used slogan was, "They say the most stressful times in life are, separation, divorce, starting a new career, and relocating. I did them all at the same time."

His desk was next to mine; the desks are stacked on top of each other so we all can listen to telephone conversations; most of them pertain to task force business, which affects us as members of the unit, so there's no guilt about eavesdropping.

The Special Agent in Command, (SAC) Ken Cloud, listened to everyone's conversations from his office; he was an eavesdropping fool. I never could figure out how he conducted his daily business while listening to task force cops and agents telephone calls.

Mike Braun received a snitch telephone call: Rick Yackey's dope courier was driving in from Fort Lauderdale with a trunk full of cocaine. He was going to off-load it at a storage facility in Wood River, Illinois. We all perked up with eavesdropped conversation. Wood River was at one time the cop/writer's home town.

We took off Yackey's dope mule and seized multiple kilos of cocaine. A kilo is approximately 2.2 pounds, so it was a sizeable seizure for Wood River, Illinois. The mule was a talker: the first words out of his mouth were, "It isn't my dope, it belongs to Paul Robinson, Dan Robinson, and Rick Yackey.

The distribution plan for this shipment was for the mule to contact Yackey and convince him that everything was okay and that he had the dope safely secured. Then Rick would tell the mule where and when to meet him with the dope.

The mule made the call; we taped it. The next day the mule drove to a fast-food restaurant on South Kingshighway in the city. The mule parked his rental car next to Yackey's junker Oldsmobile, and they exchanged cars; Yackey drove off with the dope laden rental, and the mule drove off in Yackey's junker Olds.

We took them both off on Kingshighway, arrested Yackey, seized the dope in the trunk, and turned Yackey into a super snitch. He came in on everyone, set up Paul Robinson, including a video of Paul accepting cash from Yackey.

Task Force agents arrested Paul; Dan absconded and was missing for a couple of months. One of Dan's girlfriends confided in an Egyptian she worked with at a hotel near the Lambert International Airport. Dan's girlfriend was the one who had a heroin addiction.

Dan would call her periodically and she would confide in her work friend, and he would either tell the FBI, or DEA. The FBI usually paid him for information, and DEA didn't, so it was up and down whether DEA got the information first, or the FBI. But the info would still trickle down to this cop.

On a late evening before a summer night, an FBI agent/friend, called with a telephone number. "Dan Robinson is going to be at this location at nine tonight." He hung up.

There were only two of us in the office; an issue on the telephone number headed us out to Bogey Hills Country Club Condominium Complex. The door came down easily with a sledge hammer. Inside, alone, confronted with the fugitive Dan Robinson, who wouldn't give up, fists flew, Dan was injured and was eventually taken to the hospital; he had broken ribs.

As Dan was conveyed from the hospital, to the federal lockup at the courthouse in downtown St. Louis, a conversation started. His occupation was pimp/dope smuggler/dealer, and it was apparent from his vernacular. Several of the Robinsons are pimps.

What was so inspiring to me was the fact that Dan didn't realize his pimping lifestyle wasn't working for him. He was selling himself, constantly; it was sickening. The cell door slammed shut on Dan Robinson, a sound no cop ever wants to hear from the inside. Dan stopped the pimping charade. "When my lawyer, Norm London, gets finished with you on the stand, you'll be in here and I will be out there. You handcuffed me and beat me."

"Fuck you, Dan!"

The case went to court in the Southern District of Illinois. It was super big case. On the first day of trial, Dan and Paul Robinson were sitting at the defense tables; Paul had some hillbilly hokey defense lawyer from Kentucky. He was in way over his head. Dan was sitting alone.

Norm London waltzed in with his briefcase, sat it down next to Dan and stood at the table facing judge William Stiehl, hanging judge. Assistant United States Attorney, Clifford J. Proud, former St. Louis City cop, asked for a sidebar with the judge. Both Norm and Cliff went to the Judges bench and talked in low tones.

Cliff advised Judge Stiehl that there was a possibility that Norm could be a coconspirator in a marijuana deal with the Robinsons. The $100,000 drug deal Paul Robinson ripped Norm off on. Norm did not defend himself. He turned, walked to the defense table, picked up his briefcase and exited the courtroom. Dan was left sitting alone, without an attorney. His family scrambled to get him one.

Dan got twenty years; Paul got Twenty-five. Mike Braun and the task force guys worked on this case for approximately two years. Mike was eventually promoted and transferred. He was on his way up the federal law enforcement ladder, and retired as the Director of Operations for the Drug Enforcement Administration. We stay in touch. (Details of the DEA experience can be found in the nonfiction book, Anatomy of A Federal Drug Agent.)

Nearing twenty years; a time in a nonconforming cop's life when he has to make a decision; get along with the bosses and do the rest of his/her time and get a livable pension, or venture out into the cold and try to make an honest living. A transfer to homicide swept the sweetness of DEA into the wind.

14

The ice was thin in the Homicide Section for this now crazed-cop-writer. It is common knowledge that cops coming back to reality after being in DEA or any federal cop job have a difficult time readjusting to local cop lifestyles; snitching cops, asshole bosses, weak criminal prosecution.

Homicide was structured like a line platoon in a district. Not being accustomed to structured assignments, and having been foot loose and fancy free for the past twelve years, (Intelligence and DEA Task Force) this detective was a loose cannon, a wild horse, a spring chicken; it possibly wasn't going to work. The heels of my shoes were busting through the ice as soon as the office door opened; in this cop/writer' s mind, failure was imminent.

There's camaraderie in specialized assignments. Your coworkers are your brothers and sisters. It isn't like in a district; in a district it's just you and your riding partner against the world. You hardly ever hobnob after your shift with your partner on the district level. It's just a workplace friendship.

When a cop leaves a specialized assignment, Intelligence, DEA Task Force, it's like leaving home for the Marine Corps; inside you know nothing will be like it once was; those friendships are most likely gone forever.

My friends at DEA were past friends, now. The new group, (service crew) were Sergeant Mike Guzy, and Detective Billy Qualls. The service crew was the scene first responders on a homicide. When a district cop gets a call and suspects there is a suspicious death, or homicide, he advises his precinct sergeant, and the sarge responds to the scene, and then he contacts the watch commander, and he responds to the scene, and then homicide is requested via the radio dispatcher.

Most cops in the department had heard of Guzy; we had worked together on a kidnapping murder case several years earlier. He possibly didn't remember me, but Detective Sergeant Mike Guzy makes a lasting impression, most people in and out of the police department never forget him.

He is a smart guy; graduate degree in something, not certain what it was, and he acted the part of smart guy, and carried it with him. He probably could have been something in life; doctor, or dentist, or lawyer, instead of a cop detective. The cop system is made for guys like the crazed cop; not smart but savvy, lucky to have a job with a pension.

Divorce is the terminal disease to cops. If they ever had anything in their lives, it disappears during and after a divorce. The problem with cop detectives is that if there's a problem within the marriage, or family, the cop takes the role of cop detective, instead of someone desiring to save his or her life. He usually says something askew, like, "Hey, screw you bitch, get a fucking lawyer and get the fuck out of my life."

That is what the cop wants to say to his supervisor, but he's afraid to lose his (I have arrived) status position, so he says it to his wife. Wrong tack to take, but cops do it constantly. There's no mediation after angry cop words are shot out. You can't take back words or bullets.

Guzy was working on his second marriage. Cops compare their dilemmas to other cops, and try to learn from it. The crazed cop's marriage was shaky; all cop marriages are. The wife grows to hate the police department and anything and everything attached to it, including her husband. A rational man can't blame the wife.

The police department is like a giant Anaconda digging its fangs into their beloved man, wrapping itself around his torso and systematically squeezing the life out of him. The snake allows the cop to partake of beer, cop bars, and cop buddies, if he's assigned to a specialized unit, but when it comes to quality time at home with the wife and kids, the snake squeezes until the cop can't stand it anymore.

Guzy's problems were far worse than many. As a species (cops) our problems are self-induced; attitude, arrogance, defiance of authority, (bank robbing Jimmy Cochran, and soured cop, Glen Vaughn). Some members of the species could work on those and save themselves, if they wanted to.

Guzy, and several others, were being secretly investigated by Internal Affairs for a residency violation. Cops were following them, to and from work. He had an address in the city, but his family lived outside of the city limits.

The chief we had at this time was overlooking this dilemma, but Chief Bob Scheetz (the same guy who received the information of the smuggled gun that led to the David Eugene Richardson assassination at the city jail) wouldn't be around forever, and that's when the new chief would pounce, if there were some of his enemies involved in the discretion.

Clarence Harmon became the next chief of police. Clarence was and is a good guy. He overlooked the problem, but the clock never stops ticking; it's like a condemned prisoner on death row. He can rationalize to himself, "They haven't killed me yet." But, one morning, they wake him and ask him what he wants for his last meal. The clock! Ron Henderson wanted to be the next chief, in fact he wanted to unseat Clarence Harmon.

The Board of Police Commissioners, appointed by the Governor of the Great State of Missouri, sits for four years; the members are staggered. Clarence had a political enemy; J.B. Jet Banks. He was a powerful man in the City of St. Louis and in the State of Missouri; Speaker of The House. He owned the Board of Police Commissioners. The appointees were loyal to him, not to the City, or the State. Ron Henderson was his boy.

Ron Henderson replaced Clarence Harmon. If a cop was, or had been friends with Robert Scheetz, or Clarence Harmon, then he was considered a possible enemy of Ron Henderson. We all live in glass houses; which means that if you throw rocks at my house, I will, someday, throw boulders at yours.

Cops are vocal when their guy is in command; we tend to cower like cur dogs when the other guy gets the stick. Ron had the stick; he appointed two cop sergeants, one white, Bob George, one black, Lionel Abernathy, to deeply investigate the residency requirement violations. They were relentless. It got ugly.

Both of these supervisory cops were thought of as "nice guys" throughout the police department. But they were offered an assignment by the Chief of Police. They worked out of his office; they had personal cars to drive, and to take home with them. They made their own hours. They were important!

They ruined some good cop's lives. It takes a special kind of a cop to spy on and sabotage another cop. The cops they attacked were hard working, dedicated guys. Guzy and Jimmie Carroll were just two of their victims, even though Guzy maintained his status until he was able to retire.

There are many famous cops in the St. Louis Metropolitan Police Department; none as famous as Chief of Detectives Lieutenant Colonel John Doherty, but there were some that were close to his glory. Captain George Hollocher was one of them.

Cops like Hollocher fashioned themselves after John Doherty. They would never snitch on another cop, no matter what. When a cop gets called to Internal Affairs for an infraction, or an infraction pertaining to a fellow cop, the cop on the hot seat is compelled to give a statement pertaining to the specified incident, or immediately be dismissed from the roles of the police department.

If the pressure gets too much for them, they have the option of hiring an attorney to speak in their behalf. The attorney stops the snitch fest and saves the cop's job.

One of the attorney's was Chet Pleban. He was paid by the St. Louis Metropolitan Police Officer's Association (cop union) to represent cops in trouble with IAD, Internal Affairs Division.

Chet became disillusioned with the police union and disenfranchised himself from it. He went to the other side; he was hired by the police department to assist Internal Affairs with the persecution of problem cops.

Chet was friends with several high-ranking cops. Captain George Hollocher had a conflict with Chet, and he was being investigated by IAD. George flat didn't like Chet Pleban and he couldn't hide it.

The word around the campfire (police headquarters) was that then Lieutenant Hollocher (assigned to the sixth police district as a watch commander) referred to Chet as a "pencil necked geek" to his face while being investigated for covering up a homicide in the fifth police district while on duty in the sixth. He also threatened to throw Chet out of a sixth-floor window.

These verbal actions must be taken in perspective: George Hollocher was a dedicated city cop, and had been for decades. He had rank, prestige, he'd survived combat within the city of St. Louis, which is not a given. He'd earned respect from every person he met, but he wasn't getting respect in the Internal Affairs Division on the sixth floor of police headquarters.

In George Hollocher's mind, Chet Pleban was a turncoat, leaving the police union to work with the company men at headquarters. He was a lawyer; a guy who went to law school instead of getting a job. In this mindset, Chet Pleban shouldn't even be in his presence. He wasn't worthy. George Hollocher left people like Chet lying on the street, unconscious, or dead. He was a warrior; Chet was a geek.

Cops are loyal to their civilian friends, especially friends who can help them on and off duty. City cops are all in need (unless the cop has a smart wife with a good paying job). Mechanics, construction workers, HVAC, diamond merchants, jewelers, anything a cop needs is at his disposal, but he must pay back when asked. Usually, it's getting a traffic ticket fixed, a DUI quashed, or get a relative out of jail without bail.

Mike Higgins, a roofer who lived in the fifth police district was friends with many high-ranking cops within the city police department. He put roofs on their houses, for free. He loved high ranking cops. Mike had power within the city limits. He was important. The mantra of most high-ranking cops is, "If it isn't free it isn't worth having."

Mike was having problems with a black guy who had been prowling around his house at night and burglarizing the business next door to him, Shreeves Engine Rebuilding. Mike Higgins had observed the burglar, Lewis Kincy, leaving the engine rebuilding business around midnight. Kincy was pushing a couple of tanks of welding gas and had some welding torches in his hands.

Kincy apparently ditched the welding equipment and came back to prowl around Mike Higgins' house again. Mike Higgins observed Kincy through a living room window, raised the window and grabbed Kincy by his jacket, lifting Kincy off of the ground. Kincy fought with Mike Higgins and eventually broke free of him. Mike apparently shot Kincy in the back and Kincy fell to the ground, dead, or dying.

George Hollocher was on duty as the watch commander in the sixth police district, adjacent to the fifth. Mike telephoned George at the station and told him what had transpired. George advised Mike Higgins to move the body off of his property, into the alley and near the street.

Mike Higgins dragged the body of Lewis Kincy, to a T alley intersection with Farrar Street. Someone called the police for a "shots fired" complaint and scout car 3525 responded, finding the body of Lewis Kincy.

It was a little murder, one that could have probably been deemed justifiable if investigated in its original form, but guys like Mike Higgins enjoy their fifteen minutes of fame, their hour in the sun. They cultivate hard core friendships with important cops for this reason.

But the crime went further; talk around the campfire was that George Hollocher also used his influence in the homicide section after Mike Higgins was arrested for the crime of murder. He was arrested, booked, but not charged

No problem for a friend of cops, especially high-ranking cops. This incident got out among the rank-and-file cops of the department. It was just another insane city crime to laugh and shake one's head over. It apparently was the reason for the Internal Affairs Division targeting of then Captain George Hollocher.

Had Mike Higgins accepted his good fortune, being free after committing murder, and gone on with his life, the scrutiny monsters in IAD (Internal Affairs) would have probably turned a blind eye to George Hollocher.

But guys like Mike Higgins can't do that; they brag to their beer drinking buddies about their influence within the city. It's their life; it's like a hunter bagging about a record setting deer, or a gigantic fish. Most of Mike Higgins friends were criminals. When arrested they regurgitate any criminal information made privy to them by their criminal associates, seeking leniency.

Rumors abound about city cops, especially ranking city cops. One or two rumors are noted but not acted upon. Eventually an investigation is opened on the charge of corruption. Covering up, or assisting in the cover-up of a homicide is looked down upon, depending on what side of the political spectrum you are on.

The IAD investigators, Chet Pleban, et al, could not prove the allegation against George Hollocher. Obviously, harsh words were directed at the IAD cops and Chet by George Hollocher.

George was personal friends with Commissioner John Frank. He's the guy who was at the center of the police pension fund churning incident by a lawyer friend, Don Anton, and two police pension police officer trustees, Tony Danielle, and Walter Klein, both at one time chaired the fund. Officer Danielle, Attorney Anton, and Officer Klein went to prison.

Cops, especially city cops, get a false sense of security when one of their bosom buddies becomes a police commissioner. It's a four-year gig, and the friendship blossoms during those years. The prize for the cop is multiple promotions. It appears to be what most cops are trying to achieve.

Daniele's defense was that Commissioner Frank had promised to promote him via the influence of his friend, Attorney Don Anton, and that he didn't steal anything, he just turned a blind eye to the churning of the fund and the hundreds of thousands of dollars that went into Don Anton's bank account.

Daniele eventually took Commissioner Frank hostage in his office in downtown St. Louis and held him at gunpoint for fifteen hours.

IAD waited patiently for Commissioner Frank to end his four-year term before attacking Captain George Hollocher. The bottom line was: Captain George Hollocher was going to be forced out of the department, early, and that IAD was going to use any charge available to oust him. To the casual observer this is no big deal; Captain Hollocher had a great career; he was a famous cop, had a book written about him, gained rank and esteem, why not leave with one's head held high?

Cops, in particular high-ranking cops, are cheap. The pension system is set up for longevity: 20-years, 40%, 25-years, 50%, 30-years, 75%. These figures are based on the final three years of one's employment with the police department, and cops with rank don't leave until their 65th birthday.

City cops know what their monthly stipend will be at any given year; they calculate it and manipulate the figures like an actuary, comparing ages of death of their ancestors, possible future promotions within the department, stock market predictions and personal savings.

Leaving the police department prematurely could cost the ranking cop hundreds of thousands of dollars in retirement benefits. George Hollocher balked and reacted in the only way he knew; he became aggressive and threatening; it had always worked for him.

Chet denied the "geek" rumor. He could not have cared less about Captain Hollocher's harsh words directed at him. Chet was rich and powerful. George was an important guy within the police department, but who cares about self-righteous cops? George felt he could do no wrong.

Bill McClellan (Jimmy Cochran's good friend and columnist for the socialist newspaper) wrote a non- fiction book (Evidence of Murder) about a wealthy real estate baron from New Orleans who brought his wife to St. Louis and murdered her in a downtown hotel room. The crime was first deemed an accidental injury; she allegedly slipped in the bathtub, striking her head.

George Hollocher and his partner, Steve Jacobsmeyer, both in homicide, worked the case and eventually arrested the husband, Ed Post, for the murder of Julie Post. It is a good book, and McClellan captured the personality of George Hollocher, and Steve Jacobsmeyer. They were silver screen style investigators, cocky, brash, no holds barred cops. They lived their lives off duty in the same manner.

George had a big spread in Jefferson County, Missouri, the rural county south of St. Louis. He was in violation of the police department residency requirement. George was cocky, brash, and unprotected from snitching cops. To his enemy trolls (other city cops wanting his rank for themselves) his house was not glass, it was crystal.

The lieutenant, and the top troll within the police department, (born to be an IAD investigator) joint deputy commander of the Internal Affairs Division, typically referred to as goons by the working police officers in the department, was friends with Chet Pleban. He had heard of the alleged disrespect given to Chet by George Hollocher, and he planned on vengeance for Chet. He targeted then Captain George Hollocher, hero, hard charging cop; scrutiny for cops is disaster.

It was a two-edged sword for the lieutenant troll friend of the famous attorney; he would, and did, snitch on George Holocher for being in violation of the residency rule, gain

justice for the wronged Chet Pleban, and campaign for
Holoacher's rank after he quit, or was fired for the violation.

The plan worked; George Hollocher was forced to seek
early retirement from the police department. His son, who
also worked as a civilian for the department, was also forced
out of his job. The lieutenant troll was miraculously promoted
to captain.

A few years after Hollocher's retirement, he shot his
daughter's boyfriend at his daughter's house in Barnhart. The
boyfriend allegedly physically abused her, (beat the daughter
up, badly) and the daughter told George about it.

George hid in the house until the boyfriend came back.
George came out of hiding, and the boyfriend said something
to the effect that he was going to rape George after he beat
him up, like he did his daughter. The fight was on, and George
subsequently shot the boyfriend in the neck. When two guys
fight and one of them has a gun, the guy with the gun usually
wins.

The boyfriend was bleeding profusely, and he begged
George to get him a towel to help stop the bleeding. George
provided a towel, and called the Jefferson County Sheriff's
Office. He was friends with the sheriff. It was self-defense.
Later, George told friends that he regretted giving the
boyfriend the towel.

The boyfriend went away to the state penitentiary, was
incarcerated for approximately a year, and died in prison. Old,
political, hero cops can't leave their personalities and
obsessions in the city of St. Louis when they leave.

George's wife died, and his house in Barnhart caught fire
and burned to the ground. The insurance company refused to
pay George for the burned house. George sought help from
his old friend, ex-Police Commissioner, Attorney John Frank.
The insurance company ultimately paid George for the house.

George Hollaoher passed away in 2008; a distraught victim of old-time lawman syndrome (kill the bad guy). The cop/attorney friendship between the team of Chet Pleban and the lieutenant deputy commander of Internal Affairs dissipated like an April snow storm.

During an interview of Chet Pleban for this book, Chet denied the allegation that Captain George Hollocher was targeted by IAD for the residency violation, and he further (laughingly) stated that he had probably been derogatorily referred to by many cops in the department.

He stated that Captain George Hollocher had other problems that he was targeted for; the residency violation was a minor infraction.

Make a cop feel like he's important and he will do anything his bosses tell him to do. The residency requirement was/is cruel to all parties involved, especially when the requirement is tied to racism, or cronyism.

Cop investigators interviewed neighbors, and photographed children coming and going from a St. Louis County school. Hardly any marriage could withstand that form of harassment. Orwell, what a genius! Guzy would probably be forced to resign before his twenty-year mark; a fate worse than death. But in retrospect, another divorce would totally ruin him financially, for life.

There is hidden sadness in this assault on Detective Sergeant Mike Guzy, or George Hollocher, or Jimmy Carrol; they were great cops. They all took any job seriously, and if you want a job done right, Guzy was your man. He gave 100%.

The city, the police department, they didn't care; Guzy, et al. were in violation of a department rule, a rule that was the brain trust of a railroad porter who was appointed, by the Governor of the Great State of Missouri, to the Honorable

Board of Police Commissioners in 1973; he drafted and proposed the new rule, stating all employees of the City of St. Louis Police Department must reside within the city limits of the City of St. Louis. The other members of the brain trust agreed with him. It was mandated and passed by the State of Missouri and made a law.

For as smart as he was, Guzy was a victim of ignorance, and racism. Ninety nine percent of the cops investigated, and harassed, were white. Chief Ron Henderson was black.

Had Guzy been a professional in another field, he wouldn't have had these problems. Being smart in the cop game puts the cop in the crosshairs of ranking cops who aren't smart. They hate you! Or if the cop is surly, like this cop/writer, they tap your home telephone, periodically check your savings account, or follow you when they get a chance. Crazed cop's problems were minute compared to Guzy's.

Jimmy Carroll, and his family had a special need's child; special education was not available in the City of St. Louis. Sergeant Jimmy Carroll was harassed to the extent of him leaving the department after he got twenty years on. He had to go to another police department to survive.

Cops are at the mercy of career politicians, and politically appointed police officers. It is easy to sit at the top and read a rule, and then order someone to enforce that rule. Only an ignoramus would refuse discretion.

Detective Bill Qualls came from a cop family; his dad was a retired city cop detective. He knew the ins and outs of the city cop game. "Be friends with everyone you meet. Don't make enemies. Don't call in sick. Have good stats." These are advisories every cop is told upon entering a district station for the first time. When we first hear them, we are standing in a district captain's office, (Captain Harry Lee in the bloody ninth), wearing our new uniforms, with our new nightsticks and shiny leather, hard soled shoes and a feeling of desperation. Harry Lee was a brilliant man, a military man, a deep thinker. May he rest in peace.

There is activity around us; people being manhandled, jail cell doors being slammed, telephones constantly ringing, homeless people coming and going and using the facilities, and the district stations stunk like a ghetto government rental house.

We figure Captain Harry Lee's words of wisdom didn't apply to us. We, thinking we are smart guys, instead of lucky guys, tell ourselves that we aren't going to be here for very long, so those pearls of wisdom aren't relevant. Most of us think the district police life is just temporary. Foolish boys and girls. Guys like Bill Qualls heed the advice given by their dads.

The commander of the Homicide Section was, at that time, Captain Bob Bauman. He was no Harry Lee, and this cop was on shaky ground with him. We had worked in the bloody ninth district together. The second in command was a lieutenant I had worked in Intelligence with; we were bitter enemies, and Bob Bauman and the lieutenant were office associates.

Guzy was friends with Bob Bauman; the lieutenant was friends with the Chief's Aide; a corrupt man, which gave him special power, and he would use it at his will. A bad word to the chief's aide could possibly mean a transfer to a district, a place where almost no one wanted to go. The department was all about status, job title, and rank. The commanders held your status over your head like an ancient warrior's battle axe. "People in districts want your job," was the common spiel from specialized unit commanders.

There was pressure mounting in the Homicide Section. The murders never stopped, and if you missed one, you felt lucky. The interviews of the suspects were changing; they were getting more physical. Guzy, crazed cop/writer, Qualls, we were getting short tempered, especially when the victim was a child, or gorgeous young woman. The casual observer could see the angst growing amongst us, and the other three-man crews were also experiencing it.

This cop/writer's mere presence in the section was causing turmoil. All of the detectives knew this cop was on the outs with the commanders, so he was the guy they watched, like a crowd watches an injured person trying to climb out of his overturned convertible at an intersection; it was common knowledge that if you fail in homicide, you never recover; you will be in a district for the remainder of your time on the police department.

None of us (cops) like being the center of attention for a bunch of office cops, but the game had to be played, patience applied, to see how things were going to play out for this cop, the section, and Guzy, and Qualls.

It was a strange assignment. Every cop who goes to a different assignment in a big-city police department has the same feeling, but there's always the option of making new cop friends. That option wasn't available to this cop.

Being disliked by the command personnel, most everybody in the section was leery of me. Blame? Excuses? They didn't enter to the equation. Cops make their own beds; they have to lie in them.

The homicide service crews were busy most of the time. The schedule was 6 pm to 2 am, and we rarely got off on time. Scene investigations are long and tedious, and sometimes there's an arrest which drags the overtime on. The overtime money was appreciated, but the toll on marriage and psyche was not. Guzy was a supervisor; he didn't get paid overtime.

Most of what we did was roll over the bodies of young black males, lying in the rain with their beepers going off, blood running down the street like paint from an overturned can, black looking in the street light shadows.

We rifled their pockets looking for identification, and when we found it, and when the scene was secured, and the corpse was taken away, we'd drive by the momma's house and give her the news she knew was coming, but didn't want to hear. Bad news travels fast in the African-American villages of a city like St. Louis.

The African-American villages, where sudden death is a by-product, are stuffed with gun-toting young men who will kill over a questionable word. They have no fear of death; they fear life. They expect to die violently and they accept it.

At times, we, as a service crew, would have the task of conveying witnesses to the circuit attorney's office for depositions. The street, neighborhood killers, would follow us and attempt to intimidate the witnesses. It usually worked in their favor. Witnesses were often murdered, or disappeared. Many homicides in the City of St. Louis are unsolved.

The fed had moved mid-eastern immigrants into south St. Louis City. There was an abundance of rental property there (much of it owned by city cops and firemen); Palestine, Iraq, Iran, Afghanistan, and a huge population of Bosnians were living in the old first police district. They brought baggage with them, religious baggage, cultural baggage, ignorance of the oldest type, and some of them brought hatred for America with them.

There is an apartment complex in the 3700 Block of Delor, between Spring and South Grand, that consisted of mid-eastern immigrants. While in Intelligence, some of the detectives would snoop around the complex and look for some of the residents who the FBI suspected of being terrorists living there on the government dime.

We never found anything, or anybody the fed was inquiring about; we knew there were some things the FBI didn't want to do, and they asked us to do their work for them. Mostly shots in the dark, but it was interesting to spy on possible terrorists, always intriguing, foreign espionage and spy stuff, especially when it involved the FBI.

We would park our little detective car a block away and walk to the complex, then walk around and listen and watch. We had photos of suspected terrorists with us, and at times we would compare the photos with the people we would pass.

There was always music, loud mid-east music coming from almost every apartment; music most Americans are not accustomed to, and didn't wish to be; eerie and weird sounding music; we expected to see camels dancing through the doors and onto the grassy common ground separating the buildings, and the cooking smells were non-appetizing.

We could hear people loudly speaking in Arabic, arguing and sometimes shouting, but we never found anything out for our friends at the FBI.

Being at the immigrant apartment complex was like visiting a foreign country; but in retrospect, being assigned to a black district (many were all black) was the same type of experience. Some ghetto dwellers hated America just like some of the Arabs; the African Americans had their own dialect, Ebonics, and many of them also spoke and argued with anyone within shouting distance. The cop detective job was never boring.

The service crew (crazed cop, Guzy, and Qualls) were preparing to end our shift; the last hour was always high anxiety; will we make it? The three of us had desks stacked near one another; we watched the telephone as if it was animate object, a pet or an enemy, and wondered if it would ring; it did.

Guzy answered it; "Requesting homicide at 3759 Delor, unit C," Guzy advised. We grabbed our jackets, flashlights, and legal pads and headed out. This crazed cop had been barraged with pertinent and superfluous information for the past several years, and had almost forgotten about the immigrant apartment complex; the address didn't ring a bell, but after pulling up to it, flashbacks of the Intelligence Unit investigations and the snooping around on the complex grounds attacked. Seemed like decades ago, but it had only been about four years.

We parked on the street and wormed our way toward the crowd of people standing in front of apartment C. There were approximately twenty mid-easterners blocking our way into the apartment; we ordered them to get out of our way, but they didn't. We busted through the crowd. They cursed at us in Arabic; we entered the apartment, ground floor.

Our attention was immediately directed to a partially nude young girl (Palestina Isa) lying on the floor between the kitchenette and the living room. EMS had pronounced her DOS, (dead on scene) moments before our arrival. Guzy did a close visual inspection of her; stabbed approximately six times in the chest and stomach. She had large breasts for such a young girl; one of the first responders mumbled, "Look at the size of those tits."

The girl's parents, Maria Isa, mother, and Zein Isa, step father, were handcuffed and sitting at the kitchen table. The crew glanced around the room; all of these glances, utterances, visualizations, happen quickly, maybe within five seconds of entering a murder crime scene. A sconce on the wall near the murder scene drew my attention; it would be a good place to hide a listening device. An amateur sleuth could suspect that there was a listening device in or behind the sconce.

Having had just left eight-years of cloak and daggers, smoke and mirrors law enforcement, it was difficult not to be paranoid. Cop detectives in Intelligence, and the Drug Enforcement Administration were electronically surveilled, bugged, chronicled and information is stored in some government computer.

Zein Isa was probably a terrorist; his name had been uttered by some cop, somewhere, someplace, but it was difficult to put it together; it was nagging as the scene investigation came together with Guzy and Qualls; as with all nagging utterances or innuendos, it was dismissed and replaced with the task at hand.

Police Officer Dennis Hoffman, and Police Officer Robert Sanneman, were the coppers who got the call to the apartment. Apparently, Maria Isa called to report a disturbance between she, Palestina, and Zein.

When the officers arrived, Palestina was dead on scene. Dennis Hoffman advised us that they killed their daughter during a family fight. Maria had made a spontaneous statement that the daughter had tried to knife them and that they took the knife away from her, and together, she and Zein Isa killed her.

Guzy took a closer look at the murder victim; he noted she had blood about her face, hands, arms, chest and neck, and she was lying in an apparent pool of blood under her mid-torso. There was a black handled knife near the victim's head, and a white handled knife near her torso.

Our attention was directed to the suspects, Maria and Zein Isa. We studied them trying to get a feel for them; trying to form a hypothesis so that when we interview them, we can have something to work with. If they had remorse, it could be used against them. They showed no remorse.

We looked for hatred; we didn't see any emotions from either of them; they were matter of fact, sitting hand cuffed in their kitchenette while Maria's blood daughter lay dead on the floor, by her hand, and her husband's. They would have showed more emotion if they had been watching a cop detective program on television.

Evidence technicians took photographs, seized the evidence (knives and a bloody jacket Palestina was lying on); the medical examiner called for the morgue to take Palestina's body away, and Guzy, Qualls, and me, left the scene with Officers Hoffman, and Sanneman, who had the Isa's, (Maria, and Zein) handcuffed behind their backs, walking ahead of them.

The crowd of Arabs outside of the Isa apartment had grown. There were now approximately forty angry and hostile Arabs there cursing at us and refusing to move, trying to speak to the Isa murderers, who did not speak to them.

Some in the crowd tried to stop our forward movement, or touch or interfere with us; Guzy shoved a pair of them away; the crowd started speaking loudly in Arabic. We got to our cars, and drove away from the scene. We made it to the homicide offices without being tailed or followed, took the elevator up to the fourth floor and handcuffed the Isa's to separate tables in different interview rooms. It was going to be an all-nighter.

Guzy told the crazed cop to interview Maria Isa. Qualls interviewed Zein Isa. Maria wouldn't give a statement. She spoke in pidgin English, a derivative of Portuguese, English and Arabic. It was apparent she spoke English; she made the 911 call to report the disturbance at her apartment. She was stonewalling.

The interview began, "You murdered your daughter! Do you have any feelings about that?" She stared and refused to answer. Bill Qualls had the same experience with Zein Isa. Guzy tapped on the interview office door. We conferred outside. "You doing any good?" Guzy asked.

"No, she won't make a statement."

Guzy walked away from me and advised Officers Hoffman and Sanneman to fill out booking forms and to take the pair down to prisoner processing and to book them. We finished some last minute paper work. Home time came about 0500. Got some quick sleep and was back at work the next day.

Drifted into the office about 1745; Guzy and Qualls were already there. It appeared to be a lighthearted event, coffee and smiles; the section Lieutenant was talking to them, (the troll who bushwhacked Captain George Hollocher with the assistance of Chet Pleban) motioning with his ever-present cigarette. He remarked loudly so all could hear, "Don't put Richards name in the Isa homicide report." Guzy and Qualls both had looks incredulity; the conversation stopped and the lieutenant walked away.

We began the report, crazed cop, Qualls and Guzy. The lieutenant's remark, wasn't mentioned, and the crazed cop's name was included in the scene investigation. It would have been a disaster if a defense lawyer found out one of the investigating detective's name was omitted from the report.

The Palestina Isa murder was going to be big news, worldwide. It was the first of the "honor killings" Muslims are so famous for. It was obvious that the lieutenant desired to be a part of it, even though he was at home, in bed at 0040, on November 30, 1989. The crazed cop was three months shy of his twenty-year retirement date on the police department.

The office staff and the daytime detectives drifted out of the office; our three-man service crew were sitting and talking and waiting for the phone to ring so the dispatcher could say, "Requesting homicide at……."

There was a chill amongst us; Qualls finally opened up: "You're not supposed to know this, but there was a federal listening device in the Isa apartment. The FBI listened to Maria and Zein murder their daughter. They did it because she was dating a black kid she went to school with. Zein Isa is a terrorist."

It came out quickly; the chill turned to warmth; delighted to know that years of training to be a spy wasn't a waste; once a spy……….!

"You weren't supposed to share this info with an investigator at the scene?"

"The lieutenant told us not to tell you, "Qualls advised.

This was light on the surface, but it was the starting point of the crew to emotionally separate. We had accepted each other as work friends. We drank beer together, had a few laughs, and shared a halfway trust. The section lieutenant had thrown a monkey wrench into the gears of those friendships. If the crazed cop was their friend, they would not be his friends.

Qualls wanted to be promoted to sergeant. He needed the section lieutenant for that to happen. Guzy just wanted to investigate and lock up criminals. He was already as far in rank as he desired to go within the police department. He enjoyed being, Detective Sergeant Michael Guzy, St. Louis Metropolitan Police Department, Homicide Section.

Guzy was, in his mind, an important guy. But homicide was and is a poisonous snake, always watching from its pit; the more pressure a potential victim (section member) gets heaped upon him, the closer the snake gets to striking and sinking its fangs into the stressed-out detective. The pressure was mounting, for all of us, Bob Bauman, and the section lieutenant. The murders never stop. The political games, either.

As we all suspected, and expected, the FBI released the tape of the Palestina Isa Murder. The fed didn't release it to the Homicide Section Commander, Captain Bob Bauman, they released it to the Circuit Attorney, (prosecutor) Dee Joyce Hayes.

Homicide detectives deal in death and mayhem, but we rarely hear the death throes of a victim. The tape was extremely gut wrenching. Palestina walked into the apartment and Maria and Isa were waiting for her. They argued about her boyfriend, and the fact that she had taken a job at a fast-food place near the apartment.

Zein Isa says, "Here, listen my dear daughter, do you know this is the last day? Tonight, you are going to die."

Palestina responds, "Huh?"

Zein Isa replies, "Do you know you are going to die tonight?"

Maria Isa questions Palestina about items in her book bag; in the midst of the questions, Palestina begins to shriek in fear.

"Keep still," Zein Isa loudly says to her.

"Mother, please help me," Palestina says.

"Huh, what do you mean?" Maria Isa replies.

"Help, help," Palestina says.

"What help?" Maria Isa replies.

Tina screams and Maria says, "Are you going to listen, are you going to listen?"

Screaming louder, Tina gasps: "Yes, yes, I am! Then coughs and adds, "No, please!"

Maria Isa says, "shut up!"

Palestina continues to cry, but her voice is unintelligible.

"Die, die quickly," Zein Isa says.

Palestina moans, seems to quiet, then screams one last time.

"Quiet, little one! Die my daughter, die!" Zein Isa says.

Palestina was stabbed six times in the chest with a boning knife, which pierced her heart, one lung, and liver. Zein Isa eventually admitted that he put his foot on his daughter's mouth to quiet her.

It was a big trial, Maria Isa got life in prison. She died after several years of incarceration. Zein Isa was a member of the Abu Nidal Terrorist Organization, and he and several other members were plotting to bomb the Israeli Embassy in Washington, D.C.

The FBI had bugged the Isa apartment on a F.I.S.A warrant, (United States Foreign Intelligence Surveillance Court). Zein Isa got the death penalty; he died before he could be executed.

Meanwhile, back in the Homicide Section, things weren't going splendidly for my service crew, or for the section lieutenant; he got transferred out. There were rumblings that Captain Bob Bauman was on his way out.

In a large department there were always options for those who wanted out of a specialized unit. Most cops with twenty-years on can either go up, stay put, or go out. The pension is meager at twenty-years. And if the dissatisfied cop did that, the people that he had been at odds with for years would win. Cops don't want their adversaries to win. Cops never forget their first assignment (bloody ninth district) loomed in my mind.

The plan was rundown down to the new lieutenant, Steve jacobsmeyer. We weren't enemies, in fact he was a friend. He was forthright and dedicated; not an assassin of other cops. He told me he would work on it.

A couple of days drifted by, and the bloody ninth was my new old home. The year-long recreation schedule listed work days and days off. There wasn't mayhem, and threats from supervisors, and if a supervisor didn't like a certain individual, who cares?

Intelligence detectives were forced to turn our uniforms in years earlier, so the crazed cop showed up in civilian attire. The captain, Jack Titone, wasn't particularly happy that a seasoned cop with a reputation was coming back to his district (he was no Harry Lee, either).

The young guys and gals there were trained to adhere to the "new school" ways of policing; Yes, ma'am, no, sir; don't make any waves. Just answer the radio and write parking tags and do traffic enforcement.

Some of them allowed the street people to get in their faces and smart-talk them. Never has there been such backpedaling by City of St. Louis Police Officers. We owned the streets, not the vermin who victimized the weak and weak minded. My attitude was blaring; young cops wanted to ride with me.

The crazed cop was older than dirt, as far as the other cops were concerned; forty-five years of age, surrounded by cops half his age; as old as some of their parents. It was one of the most interesting things the crazed cop has ever done.

15

The department issued new uniforms, new leather, but the old trusty nightstick hung on the left side of the utility belt. On domestic disturbance calls, the seasoned cop would at times stick his or her night stick in their belt, behind them, at an angle where it could be quickly retrieved.

The drunk, or stoned cretin who had just beaten his girlfriend, or wife, beyond recognition couldn't see it; they would get in the face of the cop answering the call, usually from a neighbor or concerned relative, and blare at the seasoned peace keeper, threatening and combative. Quick hands would retrieve the stick and street justice would be administered.

District beat cops were now allowed to wear soft soled athletic shoes; fighting is an athletic event. The shoes helped. The crazed cop was in good physical condition; better than many of the young cops. They studied the crazed cop; they had heard the stories of about the old-man-cop who gave up a job in Homicide to come back to the bloody ninth district.

Curiosity, every cop's curse (besides divorce) was haunting. Glen Vaughn came back as a failure; he wasn't seeking political peace; he was hiding at a place he didn't wish to be. Failure can't be determined until the game is played out. There were a lot of innings left in this game.

Sane cops are rational beings: Criminals are failures; people who go to penitentiaries are failures; cops trying to survive are not. But for reassurance, Jimmy Cochran's name was stuck into the department computer.

Jimmy's parole officer was contacted. He was a friendly man; he advised that Jimmy Cochran was now a Vice President of a shelving company, and that he had met a girl and had gotten married. He was straight, and successful.

That was a lot of information to chew on. Flashbacks occurred about the night the department Remington shotgun was pointed at Jimmy's head as he roared by at the stinking I-270 bridge.

Had the worm turned? Was James Leroy Cochran now the accepted member of society? Are district cops lower on the social totem pole than career criminal, bank robber, and abductor, Jimmy Cochran? He was a businessman, apparently successful.

Old district cop? Shaky career, shaky marriage, no money, working secondary for a rich kid (Adam Strauss, Hi-Tech Security) who has the backing of his millionaire stepdad, (Leon Strauss) and to add insult to injury, the kid came from gangsters.

District cops still hit the ground running, just like twenty or so years earlier. The streets hadn't changed. The people were the same, just older and more ignorant. Young cops were my partners, just like when Glen Vaughn arrived on the old squad. They were starved for detective stories.

Glen Vaughn was on the crazed cop's mind; we return home with baggage, but with our own identity, but our careers were similar. He witnessed his friend, Detective Mel Wilmoth become a murder victim. It haunted him.

In the case of the crazed cop, two cop detective coworkers took their own lives: Detective Frank Reed was in Intelligence with the crazed cop. He was a black cop, but we bonded. He eventually shot himself in the head as an Intelligence Unit sergeant (the troll form Internal Affairs Division) was kicking his door in because Frank didn't show up for work.

What would cause a police supervisor to kick in the door of a fellow cop? He had the key; he obtained it from Frank Reed's live-in girlfriend, herself a St. Louis City police department employee. She gladly gave the supervisor the key, so there would not be any forced entry.

Frank Reed hated the supervisor. The sergeant demanded that everyone love him; he was going to force Frank to respect and admire him. Frank was no sycophant; he would rather be dead than sway for an overzealous cop supervisor. Cop life in a specialized unit is tough.

Task Force Detective Johnny Reszler, was a cop friend detached the Drug Enforcement Administration. The unit detectives ran free and rampant in that job, without rules or regulations. The only rule was, "lock up dope dealers."

Johnny was hired by DEA as a special agent, went to the DEA school in Quantico and scored number two in his class. The drinking (all of us were guilty) and the prescription drugs prescribed to him by the department physician got to him. He started hallucinating, had panic attacks, lost weight, couldn't cope with daily life; he committed suicide (shot himself in the head) at his parent's house in beautiful, but deadly, north St. Louis County. Two close friends in a two-year span had the crazed cop emotionally reeling.

Leon Strauss, the guy who was restoring homes in the CWE, and the West End, had been successful in his restoration business, so successful, that he purchased the ornate and glamorous, but deserted and closed, Fox Theatre, in the 3500 block of North Grand, right down the street from St. Louis University, and near the Powell Symphony Hall.

West County people were coming back to live in the CWE, and the West End, and going to concerts at Powell Symphony Hall. Leon Strauss started an extensive and expensive restoration of The Fox Theatre. His young son Adam Strauss (adopted) assisted him in any way he could. Adam wanted to learn the restoration business; he wanted to be like his dad.

Adam had an affinity for law enforcement. Being a cop, if one doesn't need money, or comes from money, was a fool's lark. Why risk one's life for pennies when a smart guy could make millions in the real estate business?

Adam tried to stay away from the cop game, but he had befriended city cops; he knew some of them by name, rode with them, rode the horse of the cop who had the beat around his dad's house in the West End off of DeBalivere.

Adam was hooked on guns, excitement, money and power. He had the backing of his dad in whatever path he took, but being a city cop was too restrictive for a guy like him. He needed freedom, but he wanted to carry a gun and a badge.

Adam Strauss, later in life, discovered through a DNA test, that his great, great grandfather was the notorious gangster Max "Big Maxie" Greenberg. Big Maxie was a bootlegger and organized crime figure in Detroit, Michigan, and later a member of Eagans Rats in St. Louis, a murderous group of Democratically controlled union busters and thieves.

In 1919 Max "Big Maxie" Greenberg, and some other Eagans Rats, robbed the Baden Bank, 8200 North Broadway; there was a police pursuit around St. Louis; Big Maxie hid in Calvary Cemetery, just like Jimmy Cochran. Is this coincidental, or is there something in the water in St. Louis that makes criminals?

With the new inhabitants of the CWE, in and around Euclid, Maryland, Lindell, West Pine, Laclede, Forest Park Boulevard, and with the gigantic and still growing hospital complex of Barnes and Jewish, the need for extra security was mounting.

The people in the group started a neighborhood watch, which meant they would call the police at the drop of a hat, but it also meant they were having meetings and exchanging ideas on how to curb the crime, particularly in the CWE.

With the rebirth of the entertainment area in and around St. Louis University, The Fox, Powell Symphony Hall, etc. the imaginary boundaries of the CWE had moved north to Grand Avenue. The area wasn't safe then, it isn't safe now. North St. Louis is just a few blocks away.

The neighborhood watch group decided to hire off duty city police officers to patrol their neighborhoods. They placed a nice CWE lady in charge of the cops, scheduled them, and turned them loose to walk around and be seen. The money wasn't bad, but cops need to be supervised; we tend to wander if not structured by our assignment.

The experiment wasn't working. Some cops would schedule two off-duty jobs at the same time, and occasionally show up at each of them. Some cops went to prison for having two secondary jobs at once; a Sergeant had a federal government grant job, and another security job at the same time. An associate turned him in and he lost his cop job and was incarcerated in a federal prison. Greed is a poison to cops, like so many other weaknesses.

Cops from all of the districts worked the Central West End (CWE) security jobs off-duty. It was the crazed cop's schtick, walking and talking to wealthy residents, making an attempt to keep ne'er-de-wells out of the neighborhood. It was reminiscent of medieval times when the rich hired the toughest guys they could find to protect them.

In the 1920s, the Italian Mafia protected the business owners from street people; now it's university educated cops; we have no money, but we can talk a good game.

Street people and the homeless were prevalent in the bloody ninth district. There were/are homeless shelters for the street people; the Salvation Army had several care facilities; hospitals in the district could not refuse to treat the indigent because of their lack of insurance or money; the homeless took advantage of everything and everyone.

The liberal CWE residents gave to the homeless; money, food, clothing, and advice. The cops in the bloody ninth spent most of their time dealing with insane street people, or writing reports from the CWE folk who had become victims of assault, burglary, theft. It was job security for the cop who wanted to work secondary.

The secondary work paid into Social Security for the city cops. The police department did not pay Social Security; we had a pension plan. For cops who had been in the military, or worked another long- term job before becoming cops, it was wise to work secondary and gain forty quarters in Social Security.

While patrolling in the CWE, (south end) beat cops observed a young man walking a beat. He was dressed like a Royal Canadian Mounted Police Officer. A cop can see anything in the CWE, so the sight of him was dismissed as just another crazy CWE resident signifying and demonstrating event.

The next day the kid was walking in uniform again. This time he had the ninth district commander, Jack Titone, with him, walking on Euclid Avenue, smiling and talking to passersby. The young kid was Adam Strauss, and he had gone into the security business in the south end of the CWE. He hired Captain Jack Titone to assist him. He named his Security business Hi-tech Security.

It wasn't long and Hi-Tech was patrolling the entire CWE, north and south and east. Adam had some cops walking beats in the West End (across Kingshighway) also. He hired cops; the crazed cop was one of them. We started out walking, which was a good idea, then Adam Strauss started purchasing old police vehicles and restoring them for patrol duties.

Adam had a staff of office personnel, and he was making money. Each individual business was required to pony up cash for the off-duty police patrols; Adam's plan kind of worked, but when the cops went home, say at midnight, or one in the morning, the creeps would come out and steal a car, or break a business window, or rob a drunk stumbling out of a bar.

The northside criminals were accustomed to plying their trade in the CWE: their quarry was, and is today, liberal victims, most with cash in their pockets. It was their hunting ground; they did not and would not give it up. The liberal mansion owners had alarms on everything they owned, and still couldn't venture outside for an evening walk without being assaulted. People were being murdered on Euclid, McPherson, and surrounding streets.

The liberal CWE residents blamed the police, because the police had the responsibility to patrol their neighborhood. Adam beefed up the cops patrolling off-duty; working for Adam Strauss turned into a good gig, but the crimes kept occurring. Adam always had an answer for them: The cops were off duty. The cops were handling another incident in another section of the CWE.

The crazed cop was attuned to DEA, Homicide, and Intelligence; cops assigned there were strong acquaintances; many considered friends, even Mike Guzy.

With the Mafia types gone, deceased, incarcerated, the Intelligence Unit changed drastically. The detectives assigned there were now trying to identify black street gang members; a daunting task; hardly anyone knows anyone else's real name. They all have nick-names, or street names. There was no glamour or excitement there.

The DEA Task Force was no longer interesting; it was the same old rock and roll: kick in doors, beat druggies up, make them cooperate with the United States Attorney, and hardly ever see your wife or kids.

But interest in Homicide didn't wane. Being a detective in Homicide was such a flawed way to survive; cops do it because it strokes their egos. They enjoy saying "Homicide detective" assigned to the Homicide Section of the St. Louis Metropolitan Police Department.

In the bloody ninth district, the command rank cops left seasoned cops alone. There was no scrutiny, no analyzing, just show up for work and answer the radio, mainly because seasoned cops weren't seeking a promotion; just a job that could be done at work, within eight hours, and to go home at the end of their shift.

Many were decorated ex-police detectives with twenty years on the job; none of that mattered. The command rank cops were interested in the young smart cops, so they left the old cops alone.

Occasionally, cops compare where they are to where they have been; in the cop game, you're only as good as your last heroic arrest. The bloody ninth was good for the seasoned cop.

At the DEA Task Force, the Special Agent in Charge suspected some of the city cops were drug dealers. He had some of our home phones bugged, and all of the work phones tapped. Same thing in Intelligence.

That intense scrutiny was a hindrance with meaning in Homicide; scrutinized cops are and were disliked by the commander all the way down to the lowest detective. Not a healthy workplace environment for guys like Guzy and Qualls who got stuck with a detective who was facing scrutiny every day of his work place life.

Seemed like every couple of months there was a spectacular murder in old St. Louis. A guy from California

(Emory Futo) flew to St. Louis, murdered his mom, dad, and two of his brothers, and then flew back to California like nothing had ever happened. He worked at the Anheuser Busch Brewery in Southern California. He never missed a day of work in his killing spree.

Always bloody, emotional, unbelievable murders in St. Louis; This one involved two sisters from Beautiful Spanish Lake, in north St. Louis County; the home to many city cops at the time.

There is an abandoned bridge looming over the treacherous Mississippi River, connecting Missouri with Illinois. Very near where Jimmy Cochran sped by with our shotguns pointed at his big head. It is amazing on how the Mississippi River plays into almost everything tragic in the St. Louis region.

The girls, Julie and Robin Kerry, twenty and nineteen, cute and perky, smart and religious, took their vacationing cousin, nineteen-year-old Thomas Cummins from Maryland, a Washington, D.C. suburb, to the bridge; it was a neat place to view the Mississippi where it makes its confluence with the Missouri, and then heads south toward downtown St. Louis, and to the deep south. Scenic and deadly. If you are on the bridge you are at the mercy of any drugged, sexual-psychopath who is also on the bridge.

The three of them bumped into a group of youngsters, like them, enjoying the late-night views, Marlin Gray, Antonio Richardson, Reginald Clemmons, and Daniel Winfrey. Daniel Winfrey was fifteen and the only white kid in the assault group; the rest were in their later teens.

Marlin Gray, at nineteen was the oldest of the group, he showed the Kerry sisters, and their cousin, Thomas Cummins, how to climb down through a manhole and stand on one of the bridge piers to get a better look at the river. Marlin then went back to his car and smoked marijuana. He told one of his group that he "felt like hurting someone tonight." The four men raped the Kerry siters and then tossed them off of the pier into the turbulent waters of the nasty Mississippi River. They were going to kill Thomas Cummins, but he jumped into the water.

Thomas Cummins survived the leap into the Mississippi River. The Kerry sisters did not. Cummins swam to shore and walked along Riverview Drive, (a nasty, dangerous thoroughfare linking the nasty city with equally as nasty, north county) trying to stop cars begging for help. Someone called the city cops, and a patrol car eventually picked Tom Cummins up.

Tom relayed his story to the cops, they called their supervisor, he called Homicide. Detectives Ray Ghrist, and Gary Stittum were dispatched to the area of Riverview and Hall Street. Ironically, Gary Stittum lived just a stone's throw from that intersection. Ray Ghrist lived just a little further on Bellefontaine Road. They were essentially in their own back yards. The two bridges, (new one and old one) were parts of their lives.

The fire department was called to help with the search of the river bank for the Kerry sisters. The Coast Guard patrolled the shore from the river looking for them. Their search was to no avail; it was dark and the Mississippi River is unforgiving that close to the confluence of the Missouri and the Mississippi.

Tom Cummins ended up in a Homicide Section interrogation room, injured, (fractured hip), muddied by Mississippi River toxic mud, and confused. The day watch detectives came in. Captain Bob Bauman was a hands-off commander; it is the frame of mind ineffectual cops get when they become commanders of a specialized unit, especially Homicide.

The deputy commander, Lieutenant Steve Jacobsmeyer, crazed cop's friend, and a friend to most cops, was vocal and energetic, and seemed like a natural to be a boss in the Homicide Section. His dad was a Lieutenant Colonel in the police department, and his uncle was the commander of the Homicide Section for most of Steve's young life. Steve was cop royalty. He grew up hearing cop stories, and murder stories. He was an expert investigator before he was out of high school.

Detective Sergeant Mike Guzy was on the day watch. Detectives Ghrist and Stittum, were due to get off at 0200, but they were still there trying to get the story straight so they could write something and go home. They verbally relayed the Kerry sister's murders, and the story of Tom Cummins to Guzy and Jacobsmeyer, and were told to go home by Jacobsmeyer. They left the offices, gladly. Tom Cummins wasn't as lucky.

Lieutenant Jacobsmeyer and Sergeant Guzy discussed the statement by Tom Cummins; they didn't believe him. Jacobsmeyer checked a Chain of Rocks Bridge stat; "The bridge is eighty feet above the Mississippi River at that location," Jake advised Guzy. "Nobody could survive that fall. He's lying." Actually, where Tom jumped into the nasty Mississippi River, the bridge was less than fifty feet from the water.

Guzy was enamored by Steve jacobsmeyer; almost everyone in the department was. Not only with his lineage, but the guy was a hero among cops. He was shot in the line of duty. He climbed through the ranks quickly; the Chief of Police, Bob Scheetz loved him more than he did his own sons. Steve was destined to take over from Captain Bob Bauman.

Steve Jacobsmeyer was a German St. Patrick who rid Ireland of snakes; he could do no wrong.

The day watch detectives started interrogating young Tom Cummins. Lieutenant Steve Jacobsmeyer assisted Guzy's crew in their line of attack, standing outside of the interrogation room and giving them new insight on how to break this terrible murderer of these beautiful young girls; his own cousins. "He did it because he wanted to have sex with them," Steve rambled on. "They turned him down, and he tossed them off of the bridge. He did it, keep on him, he'll break."

The hammering of Tom Cummins lasted for thirty-six hours. Tom eventually said, "okay, whatever you guys say, just leave me alone. Steve Jacobsmeyer said, "Bingo, we've got a confession." He ordered Detective Chris Pappas to take Tom Cummins over to the department video section to have a confession video made. Tom refused to make the video.

A relative finally called a criminal defense lawyer, Frank "Tony" Fabbri. Fabbri waltzed into the Homicide offices and demanded to see his client. Tom was on the verge of passing out; Fabbri looked at him, "It's over, Tom, the interrogation is over," Fabbri said. "Do not make another statement. Do not say another word. Do you hear me?"

"Yes, sir," Tom muttered.

Tom Cummins was booked for two counts of first-degree murder. The detectives took the case to Assistant Circuit Attorney, Nells Moss. Moss refused to issue a warrant against Tom Cummins. There was no evidence showing that Tom murdered the Kerry sisters. Tom was released.

There's was evidence on the bridge; a Kell flashlight, the kind cops use, and can also be used as a fighting tool. They have serial numbers on them, and some are listed in the Kell company files as who owned, or purchased the flashlight.

Two city Homicide detectives, Trevor and Brauer, called the Kell company and were advised who had purchased the flashlight. It belonged to a cop who lived in north St. Louis County. They asked him about the light, which had his last name engraved on it; HORN. Also engraved on it was the name Antonio.

The North County cop advised the detectives that the flashlight had been stolen from his house, and that he suspected that Antonio Richardson, a neighborhood kid, had stolen it in a burglary of his house.

Detectives Trevor and Brauer went to Antonio Richardson's apartment and rousted him. Antonio told them what they wanted to hear, indicating that he didn't rape or murder anyone, but that Marlin Gray and the others did. It broke the case.

Marlin Gray was eventually executed by the State of Missouri. Daniel Winfrey testified against all of them. Antonio Richardson, Reginald Clemons, got life. Daniel Winfrey got thirty years, did fifteen and got out.

The crazed cop watched this case unfold from the safety of the bloody ninth district. Captain Bob Bauman, or any of the other Homicide supervisors did not have access to old bloody ninth district cops seeking refuge. They controlled and scrutinized homicide dicks.

It was the luck of the Irish for the crazed cop not being in the Homicide Section when this Chain of Rocks Bridge fiasco occurred. It would have been nearly impossible to not have been one of the interrogators of this kid, Tom Cummins.

The interrogation got big press coverage in the liberal/socialist newspaper, The St. Louis Post Dispatch; liberal newspaper for a liberal city. Someone would have to take the responsibility for the thirty-six-hour interrogation of an innocent man. It was Captain Bob Bauman. He was shipped to the bloody ninth district. He brought Detective Sergeant Mike Guzy with him.

Guzy was a respected work associate; being in his presence was uncomfortable. He was too intense for a casual cop to be around. Luckily, for the crazed cop, Guzy was put in charge of the detective bureau in the bloody ninth. He had a group of willing detectives to supervise.

Several months later, Frank "Tony" Fabbri, was arrested and charged federally for stealing drug-client cash from the government. He was supposed to turn in some forfeited cash to the court in the Southern District of Illinois; the pot was light; his client turned against him; he was incarcerated in Leavenworth, disbarred, and ruined. Tony Fabbri was in reality, a good guy, and he loved cops.

Lieutenant Steve Jacobsmeyer was eventually promoted to Captain. He was forced to take an early retirement after allegations of spousal abuse, and the alleged assault of a girlfriend. The cop prodigy sells real estate.

16

Adam Struss was becoming a success in the ornate, historical, gorgeous Central West End of sleepy old St. Louis, Missouri; the stats (robbery and assault) had changed, but we're still the murder capital of the United States of America, and the CWE was still a dangerous place to be.

There was need there; need for security; need for police presence; need for cops to make extra money, for city cops were always in need of secondary employment; it's how they fed their families, took vacations, purchased that new second hand vehicle.

Adam Strauss had all of this information about cops, and cop employment. It seemed like the residents of the St. Louis city limits, knew everything about city cops. As we drive around the city neighborhoods, within ourselves, inside of the cop car, wondering about things that are important to us; family, vacations, money, schooling for our children, we tend to think we are an island, that no one knows us, and that we are the silent warriors protecting the masses for eight hours, only visible when we are needed.

But that isn't the case. Everyone we see has the inside information on us. We, as a group, are discussed, scrutinized, analyzed and pigeonholed. We are the servants of the wealthy liberals in places like the CWE; laborers with a gun and a badge. The trick is; how can the liberals use this batch of slow learners (city cops) to their advantage? We are also servants to the poor.

Adam had the equation. He didn't learn it from conversation, or by going to college, he learned about city cops through osmosis. He studied them from afar, and then got close to them. Coupled with the information tossed about by his dad, and his dad's wealthy CWE friends, Adam was able to form a hypothesis about city cops, a real-life correspondence course called "How to manipulate city cops, 101!". It worked to his advantage.

All cops start at the bottom of the organization; some cops (like Glen Vaughn and the crazed cop) start at the bottom, work our way up to glory status, and then work our back to the bottom.

Adam acquired security contracts with the CWE neighborhood organizations, north of Lindell and south of Lindell. He had an abundance of cops working for him; he was their Chief of Police while they worked off-duty.

Adam rode around the CWE in his unmarked detective looking car (a Chevy Impala Super Sport with a Corvette engine). He had a red portable dash light, just like Tom Rangel and the other detectives had when we were big-shot detectives in Intelligence.

When Adam wanted to act like a real cop, he'd throw the red revolving light on the dash and floor the Super Sport. He was licensed by the Honorable Board of Police Commissioners as an armed security officer; he carried a badge and a gun. He was gun-happy.

One of Adam's biggest ego trips was having a uniformed officer ride with him in his hotrod Chevy while he acted out television cop/crook series screenplays and sped around the Central West End, the west end, and eventually around his dad's theatre in midtown (Grand and Washington). He was always smiling; the cops looked bewildered, like Jimmy Cochran's hostages, but the cops needed the money; Adam had it; we're whores for most everyone, especially in a town like St. Louis, liberal, tight, socially structured.

In some affluent communities, the elite (CWE types) neighborhoods are occupied by staunch conservatives; not so in old St. Louis, the elite here are bleeding heart liberals (for the most part). The CWE libs would view Adam with the stoic cop riding shotgun, depressed looking, in uniform, while Adam dressed like an undercover Intelligence Unit detective, driving up and down their streets. It was part of the show; Chief Adam and his band of not so merry cops. We (cops) were trapped like rats.

The next step for Adam was credibility; he needed it. He had to get the old city cops to respect him, and maybe even like him. Money helped, but money only rents respect, it doesn't buy it. He had the bloody ninth district commander, Captain Jack Titone on his payroll; rumor was Captain Jack was his partner in the security business.

 But Jack Titone took an early retirement from the city police department; he was now the Chief of Security for St. Louis University. For a city cop, being hired by St. Louis University was like being invited to guard the Vatican. It was big-time prestigious. Bob Bauman and Mike Guzy took his place (it took two of them).

Lieutenant George (Guido) Venegoni, a paisano of Jack Titone, worked all of the secondary employment he could get. He was a motivated, smart guy, and he worked for Adam Strauss. Take into consideration, Adam Strauss had very little formal education outside of High School. He had a feel for things relating to business; he was offhand, off-cuff, and off the top of his head; he had a knack, and the security business is just like every business; you need good, reliable, smart people to be in charge of employees; in this instance, cops.

Adam Strauss hired Lieutenant George Venegoni. George was the guy who made the monthly schedules of the cops who worked the secondary shifts. He was a salaried employee of Hi-Tech Security. People/cops, trusted and respected George Venegoni. He didn't have a reputation of the kind of supervisor who tried to screw over a beat cop. He was and is intelligent.

George diligently and meticulously made the monthly work schedules. He would telephone the secondary cops and ask them what and when they wished to work. This tactic helped make Adam Strauss a successful businessman, and Adam was successful. He had contracts all over the city for secondary cops to patrol the city neighborhoods.

There was always a problem in St. Louis, in nightclub, or restaurant districts, with customers being accosted after a night of dining or drinking while going to their cars. Black criminals ruined Gaslight Square; it tainted the CWE, it closed the Debalivere Neighborhood, north of Forest Park. Which at one time had fine restaurants, a movie theater, and nightclubs.

Street creatures lay in wait for debilitated victims to wander in the dark, aimlessly, unprotected, trying to find their cars. They are the perfect victims. They can't (in most cases) give a description of the person who beat them, robbed them, raped their wives or girlfriends while someone stood with a gun to their head. It is a terrorist tactic used by street criminals who hate free enterprise, and feel entitled to be criminals.

Neighborhoods like the CWE, the West End, Soulard, The Grove, Washington Avenue (East and West), The Hill, Cherokee Street, hired some sort of outside security, as well as some residential neighborhoods. The city was, and is, a snake pit of criminals waiting to pounce on any unsuspecting soul. Bad for business, but extra security gave the business owners the opportunity to say, "Hey, I hired security, off duty St. Louis cops. Where were they when this lady got raped and robbed, and her boyfriend was shot and killed?"

Adam lived his dream, he had St. Louis cops as friends. Some cops worshipped him. He was everything some cops wished they were; accepted, respected, wealthy, connected, and adopted by a kind Jewish developer, real-estate baron, and influential man.

And to think, Adam was able to start this prosperous security company, from scratch, and he never set foot in a college. The cops were (at that time) expected to go to college. A junior college degree was required.

City cops would toil over homework, tests, going to class after working all night, fighting sleep in those stupid classes; but the city paid for most of it. We were all indoctrinated to gain college degrees. Some cops got master's degrees, Doctorates.

It didn't help them (in most cases) but there was the "what if factor"; what if I got an influential friend who would talk up for me? I could get promoted. "What if" I could get hired by the feds? In most cases it was all for naught. Adam had the inside information. He was brilliant without wasting time and money. Cops eventually realized, and accepted his success.

Ron Hasty, a bloody ninth district cop, loved Adam Strauss like a brother. Ron was a hard charging, super cop. He had a knack for being at the right place at the right time, and he had a need for extra cash. He worked secondary employment whenever he could. Adam used him for any security detail he could. Some of Adam's security jobs might require one cop for an evening, maybe at a function in the west end at one of the mansions. Adam used cops; cops used Adam.

Adam would get security requests from all over the city. Short term security details made money for Adam, and the cops he hired. Ron Hasty was one of the best. He never let Adam down; he was punctual, dependable, and loyal; just what every rich-kid businessman from the CWE wishes for.

Ron was so enamored with Adam Strauss, he asked Adam to be a godfather for one of his children. Adam put him off, but Ron was persistent. He had the ceremony set up with his parish priest, and he told Adam what he had done. Adam was still hesitant, and Ron asked him why.

"I'm Jewish," Adam replied. "What if the priest finds out I'm Jewish. He's not going to allow your child to have me as a godfather. He'll be talking about how the Jews killed Jesus, and stuff like, that. It will be embarrassing for me, you, and the priest, and maybe even your infant child when he becomes an adult."

"He won't know it," Ron replied. "Just go through with the ceremony, please."

"Okay", Adam replied. The ceremony went on without a hitch. Ron Hasty and Adam Strauss had a long and prosperous friendship. Regretfully, Ron was forced to take an early retirement from the St. Louis Metropolitan Police Department.

Ron posted something benign on Facebook that was interpreted as "racist" by the new liberal regime of the City of St. Louis. They forced a great cop out of the business.

Detective Pete Gober was a famous cop detective. Pete worked in the Intelligence Unit in the 80s. His partner, as is often the case, and Pete became bitter enemies, (Pete stuck a .38 snub revolver in his partner's stomach and told him he would kill him, in a bar, in downtown St. Louis).

Pete was a bubble off, and he was a killer. He could have, and would have, killed his partner in the bar in front of dozens of witnesses. Pete was transferred to the DEA Task Force; the partner desired power within the police department; he wanted rank, and he got it, retiring as a Major.

DEA Task Force gigs only lasted three or four years, and then it was back to the police department. Pete didn't want to come back; his old partner was waiting for him with rank and power, so Pete scrambled to find a new home within law enforcement.

The Task Force did a lot of drug work in Jefferson County, Missouri. Country folk were selling cocaine to anyone who desired it. Marijuana was prevalent for almost everyone. A lot of the marijuana and cocaine was being smuggled in by Dan Robinson (resident of Imperial, Jefferson County, Missouri), and given to the country folks on consignment. The local cops in the many municipalities would get information on the local druggies, and call the DEA Task Force. If there was a substantial cash seizure, the police department would get part of the proceeds.

Pete did his twenty years, was transferred back to the police department, but didn't show up. He took a job with Pevely, Missouri (Jefferson County) Police Department, located in rural, but beautiful Pevely, Missouri. He divorced his terminally ill wife, and married a gorgeous gal who worked in the Homicide Offices. She was most cops dream girl; some even had photos of her on their desks. But she married Pete, and they moved to rural Pevely.

Pete was a gregarious fellow; big man (obese) and big personality. He desired rank within the Pevely Police Department, but not within the City of St. Louis Police Department. He became a Lieutenant in Pevely. But he was still a cop, and he needed more money to support his cute wife. He became friends with Adam Strauss, and worked for him off-duty.

Adam was a beggar for cop friends; he couldn't get enough of them; they excited him, intrigued him, and if they had a resume (like Pete Gober) they were endeared to him. Pete was one of Adam's special cop friends, and he gave Pete special assignments, and jobs, just to keep him working and making money.

Pete returned the favors bequest upon him by Adam. Pete got Adam a part time cop job in Pevely; that sounds benign on the surface, but it meant that Adam was now a full- fledged cop in the State of Missouri, and certified as such. He could now carry a badge and a gun anywhere in the state, and he had arrest powers.

A St. Louisan coming back from the boot heel could observe Adam's hot rod Chevy Impala on the side of the road on I-55; Adam inside with a radar gun, and a dashboard red light. If a car was speeding, maybe ten miles per hour over the limit, Adam would take off after them. Adam was justifying his existence as a Pevely cop.

Pete Gober was ill; he needed a heart transplant and he was off-duty. Adam still paid him to dispatch for him, but Adam's longevity at Pevely was in peril. Adam did not wish to give up his commission as a cop in Pevely. It meant a lot to him. His dream in life.

Adam had purchased two duplex style homes in the 4000 block of Laclede; he lived in one and was rehabbing the other one. The one he lived in was also the headquarters for his security business. It's where the cops went when they reported for duty.

There was a makeshift command center set-up there, and a radio, and a dispatcher. He eventually purchased a dilapidated building on South Vandeventer, south of Manchester; the property had an outbuilding for maintenance on his junky recycled police cars, and lots of parking for the vehicles during the daytime hours.

At the height of Hi-Tech Security, Adam had contracts with six special business districts in the Central West End (bloody ninth district). With the Washington University Medical

Center, they formed the Neighborhood Security Initiative in 2007. Hi-Tech was knocking down over a half million a year just from these contracts. Adam had approximately 100 city cops working for him; most of them were his friends. He was in cop junkie heaven.

On May, 13, 2008, a Chicago resident, Tom Dobrowski, and his son, a student at St. Louis University, were sightseeing on Westmoreland Place in the CWE. It was after midnight, and that area is private. The homes are the typical 1900s World Fair style homes that made St. Louis famous, worldwide. Massive, brick, ten- bedroom mansions, five air conditioners, three or four furnaces. The kind of homes Adam Strauss grew up in. It's where the world-famous Mark and Patricia McCloskey live, the man and wife who defended their property with a pistol and a military rifle from trespassing, violent protestors in 2020.

Hi-Tech Security had the security contract to guard the area. The security guard stopped the Dobrowski's and advised them the area was private. He attempted to detain them so he could call Adam Strauss and have him come to the location. Someone allegedly punched the security guard.

The security guard (not a police officer) screamed for help on the radio; to a city cop, or to Adam Strauss, that was like yelling "FREE FOOD" to a starving man; they came in droves.

The Drobowski's were in the process of leaving, cops in security company vehicles swarmed the Drobowski's vehicle, guns were being flourished at them as they attempted to drive away from the scene.

A guy in a BMW (Adam Strauss) with a red light on his dashboard, and a female riding shotgun (both in plain clothes) pulled alongside of the Dobrowski's and pointed Glock semiautomatic pistols at them; they pulled over.

The Drobowski's were on the telephone with a 911 dispatcher. Everything said during the pursuit and the eventual detainment was being recorded by the 911 dispatcher.

A male voice said, "pull them out, everybody in a Hi-Tech car is a cop! Hellooo! Your mistake!" The Drobowski's paid a $100.00 fine for trespassing. There was a Police Board trial for Adam; a member of the Cathedral Square Business District said he suspected Hi-Tech of "double dipping" by having one officer covering two districts.

Gary Wiegart, at the time the President of the socialist police union, was not a friend of Hi-Tech Security, or Adam Strauss. He resented the city cops who worked for Adam, and he resented Adam Strauss. Wiegart went on record saying, "Do you really want the power of policing to go to a private company? I'm against people paying taxes for services that should be provided to them in the first place."

Groups of citizens monitored Hi-Tech security guards, following them and noting where they went, and how they patrolled. If a Hi-Tech cop ventured out of his assigned area, it was noted and brought to the attention of Adam Strauss, or Lieutenant George Venegoni.

Adam Strauss was stripped of his security license by the Honorable Board of Police Commissioners; (honorable because they say they are) he could still operate his business, but he was no longer a plainclothes armed security guard.

But he was still a part time cop in Pevely, Missouri population 5,873. He was Pevely's traffic division; it didn't cost Pevely any money; he provided his own vehicle, his privately owned radar gun, and he even paid for the book of traffic tickets. This was the beginning of the end for Hi-Tech Security.

It was also the end of Adam Straus' reign of power in St. Louis. He was being scrutinized by the powers that be; St. Louis hierarchy, cops and politicians. He had had a good run; twenty years of fighting crime in his own neighborhood, and elsewhere. He still had his guns, and he wore them proudly, everywhere, with his Pevely Police Department badge attached to his waist near his Glock semi-automatic pistol.

Dobrowski made a statement after paying the fines for himself, and his son; he compared St. Louis to a communist state. Not quite communist, Mr. Dobrowski, but you have great insight; the free enterprise system is faulted here.

Cops, especially high-ranking cops, don't like being beaten at their own game. Adam was doing that. He was besting the hierarchy of the St. Louis Metropolitan Police Department, and he was gaining power; he had the hearts and minds of 100 City of St. Louis Police officers.

Adam took nothing and turned it into a thriving business. He had hardly no inventory or overhead; his product is, was, City of St. Louis police officers. He was taking the product of the City of St. Louis and using it to become wealthy; free enterprise! He was setting himself up for an attack of gigantic proportions.

Ego freak ranking cops don't like being looked over. He could have paid some of them off; many would have accepted a bribe to not hate him, or attack him. In the cop/crook game, money talks, bullshit walks.

There is a cyber investigation unit within the St. Louis Metropolitan Police Department. The city pays big-money to send these computer savvy cops to schools. Federal schools. They come back to the police department with the cyber ability to snoop on someone's computer, or cell phone.

The police sergeant in charge of this section disliked Adam Strauss. Why? You may ask; jealousy, probably. Adam was born rich, never did anything in his life to warrant his success; his success was a fluke, at best. He was playing a game of cops and robbers and Voila, he's rolling in cash, and fame. Everybody knows his name; It is what cops strive for, but they're always in the background (except John Doherty).

So, a deputy chief, or a major within the police department, approaches the guy who hates Adam Strauss (the guy in charge of the computer hacker cops), and says something to the effect, "Vet this guy Adam Strauss for me. I will help you with a promotion down the line.")

The cyber section sergeant tells one of his hackers to periodically snoop on Adam's electronic toys. The trained hacker starts his attack on the privacy of Adam Strauss, illegally. But it doesn't matter; nobody will ever know, not even Adam.

17

Criminals are equal opportunity creatures; if a crime works for one of them, others will follow. They go to extreme measures to not get caught, but most do. "They never let you down"; cops use this phrase almost every day of their lives. Crooks do stupid things, but when a crime is successful, and for years goes unsolved, cops scratch their heads and wonder, who was slick enough to pull this off?

Nora Attaway was a 25-year-old college graduate who, in 1991, made the fatal mistake of coming to St Louis, Missouri to further her education. She was smart, ambitious, and nice looking. She rented an apartment in Dogtown, a neighborhood west of Forest Park, about a mile south west of the CWE, as the crow flies, if it flies off from the roof top of the world-famous Chase Park Plaza Hotel.

Nora was accosted inside of her apartment; a cretin crawled through her bedroom window, beat her and strangled her, raped her as she was dying, and slinked away into the darkness. He left his calling card (a lone fingerprint on a light bulb) he unscrewed before the deadly assault. The case was cold; almost a year went by and there was no arrest, or leads, just the lone fingerprint.

There is an abundance of history in St. Louis, and much of it is stored, or displayed in and around the CWE, Forest Park corridor. The Missouri History Museum, the Art Gallery, Washington University archives, St. Louis University library; history abounds for those who wish to pursue it.

Regrettably, neighborhood bars also are in abundance. It's almost a "rite of passage" within the city limits to frequent a neighborhood bar. Again, everybody knows your name, etc. It's the hobby of many bewildered St. Louisans.

Joe Vetrone, a mountain of a man, who resembles a grizzly bear, pursued the St. Louis dream; hang out, drink beer, and be independent. It's not that Joe wasn't smart; he was. He has a bachelor's degree in Visual Arts from a notable university.

Joe didn't pursue the success of his degree after graduation, most of us do not; Joe was, and is, a bouncer at the Pageant, a concert venue in the City of St. Louis, just east of University City, attached to Washington University. His size was intimidating to most sane humans, but not all of us.

Joe was drinking in one of his haunts; a squirrelly, and small in stature young man, picked a fight with him. Joe could have squashed him like a cockroach, but Joe kept his cool. The squirrel wouldn't back off; someone called the cops.

Cops don't wish to be bothered with such trivialities, so they tried to turn the event into a peaceable result. The squirrel wouldn't have it; they arrested the squirrel; Joe was given a summons to appear in court.

The squirrel, Hunter Ford, was, and is, the adopted son of Dick Ford, at one time a charismatic television newsman. As in all official arrests, Hunter Ford was processed; fingerprinted, photographed, and placed in a holdover cell where he could make bond, or spend twenty hours before being released.

His fingerprint on the lightbulb he unscrewed before he beat, raped, and murdered Nora Attaway, his murderous calling card, came back to haunt him. Homicide detectives pounced on him; he was interrogated; he confessed to the horrendous crime. He was incarcerated for life, without the chance of parole. They never let you down.

In 1992, a couple of slick crooks robbed an armored car picking up cash at the United Missouri Bank in downtown St. Louis. Brinks guard, Clyde Blakey, took a freight elevator to the basement of the bank, and picked up bills of varying denominations stuffed in five bags. He was to take the money to the Federal Reserve Bank downtown, just about five blocks from United Missouri Bank.

While pushing the bags down a hallway on a cart, he was stopped by a masked man armed with a revolver. The armed man, with an accomplice, tied Blakey up with rope and tape; one of the robbers spoke in whispers, the other one did not speak. They got away with $847,000.

Every cop, security official (Adam Strauss) and federal agent in the region was trying to solve this robbery. There were snitches working overtime, some seeking a reward, some working off drug, and other pending cases.

The solving of the daring armored car robbery in beautiful downtown St. Louis, in the shadow of the government idol, (The Arch) would be a feather in the cap of anyone who had the information to solve it. Somebody knows who robbed the Brinks guard. Why aren't they talking?

The crazed cop had information on it; a call to City Intelligence, (his old home) was fruitless; the commander there at the time cursed at the crazed cop over the phone and ordered him to never telephone his bureau again.

The city cops and the FBI worked tirelessly, but it was never solved. In 1999, a U.S. Armored Car Services van was robbed in Hazelwood, Missouri (beautiful north county), the robbers walked away with one million. Never solved.

The Brinks crime, and the U.S Armored Car robbery was, and is, what crime dreams are made of. Regular street criminals, like the ones who terrorize the liberals in the CWE, the ones Adam Strauss had sworn to protect and serve, with the help of off-duty cops, feel entitled to the "big score."

One of the problems with a crime like the United Missouri Bank, Brinks guard, robbery is, so many law enforcement folks deeply feel they know who did it. Guys in the FBI, City Intelligence, Burglary and Robbery in the Bureau of

Investigation, know every professional crook in the region. They know them on sight, their friends, their relatives, their girlfriends and where they consume alcohol, or shoot dope.

The cops and agents, within themselves, feel their quarry is laughing at them for not catching them. Crime is a game, until one gets caught.

So, what if the Brinks, United Missouri Bank robbery wasn't committed by professionals? That is a terrifying problem to law enforcement. It means ordinary people are capable of committing successful money-making crimes. It takes guts, and desperation to commit a crime like this.

Jimmy Cochran did it, several times, and got caught almost every time. The odds of a guy like Jimmy Cochran being successful at daytime bank robbery are small. Somebody, quite possibly an amateur, did the improbable.

The Grand Center Entertainment District, in the belly of the bloody ninth district, squared by Grand, Lindell, Spring, and Delmar, is the focal point of high-end entertainment in the St. Louis region.

The area contains the Contemporary Art Museum, the Fabulous Fox Theater, The Grandel Theater, The Kranzberg Arts Center, The Metro Theater Company, Portfolio Gallery and Educational Center, Powell Symphony Hall, Pulitzer Foundation for The Arts, Sheldon Concert Hall, Sun Theater, The Harold and Dorothy Steward Center for Jazz, and the Vaughn Cultural Center.

Off duty cops are hired by the Cultural Arts Center to guard the patrons coming and going, and to ensure their cars are not stolen, or vandalized. Anything left unattended will be plundered.

Tucked amidst the cultural paradise, on the fringe of the north St. Louis African American village, shielded only by the United States Veterans Hospital to the north, is the ATM

Solutions Company, 3721 Grandel Square, across the street from the historic Sun Theater. There is no sign on the gray, nondescript masonry building, and the hundreds of northside residents who drove or walked past it daily would not know that there was big cash inside, waiting to be pilfered.

Desperate folks talk about big scores. Many are criminals, not lucky ones, for it seems that the poorer they are, the more they fail at crime.

North siders are infamous crooks. Four area guys, Rychene Money, John Wesley Jones, Larry Newman, and Aaron Hassan Johnson, had a friend who was at one time an employee at ATM Solutions.

The company serviced ATM machines in the St. Louis area. The security guards, and armored van drivers, stuffed cash into the machines at banks and other locations.

The one-time employee advised Rychene Money of the procedures at ATM, the hours when the personnel showed up for work, how it took two employees to unlock the vault, and how the employees were staggered at their time for shift duty; Rychene started thinking about the possible robbery of ATM Solutions.

A little information, like a little money, is a dangerous thing. Street crooks aren't Rhodes scholars; not even smart criminals are in reality, smart. Rychene made his first mistake: he enlisted the help of other small-time crooks to join him in the caper. These guys were the types of criminals who robbed liberal white folks in the CWE.

A few of them started out sucker punching old ladies and feeble men who were shopping in Maryland Plaza. In St. Louis, if a person shows the slightest bit of weakness, he's identified as a potential victim by people like Rychene and his band of ATM Solutions robbers.

Historically, successful armored car robberies, or bank robberies, have no more than two or three perpetrators. Crooks talk; they brag about their scores to their paramours, their relatives; they are proud of their achievement. Only professional crooks, or damned lucky amateurs, get away clean.

So, Rychene and his crew set out to attack and rob ATM Solutions on historic Grandel Square, right in the belly of the bloody ninth district. At daybreak, dressed in black, with face coverings, and armed with semiautomatic military rifles, and pistols, this haphazard crew of knucklehead misfits forced their way into the compound after overpowering a guard, the first on duty guard of the day. They knew it took two guards to punch in the security codes to open the vault. There were surveillance cameras everywhere; the robbers were on television and being recorded.

They got into the vault and stole as much as they could in the small amount of time they had allotted themselves. The mistakes began: The cash they were stealing was mostly 10s and 20s. It weighed over 1000 pounds. They had all come in one car, an old Pontiac Grand Prix. They were forced to steal one of the ATM Solutions vans to transport the cash to their scrub home on Page Avenue, about four blocks away from the scene.

They loaded the van with the help of the two security guards. They tied up the guards with duct tape, and locked them in the vault, drove away in the van and the Grand Prix. The score was 6.6 million dollars. Biggest score in bank robbing history in sleepy old, criminal, St. Louis, Missouri.

They unloaded the cash from the armored van at a residence on Page Avenue, then abandoned the van in the 4400 block of Evans, about two miles from ATM Solutions, an all-black, old time, St. Louis neighborhood where everyone knows everyone, and everyone is in fear of one another. Death is the reward for any confrontation in these neighborhoods.

Approximately ninety minutes after the robbery, a police officer patrolling on Evans spotted the van. FBI and city cops swarmed the area. There was a witness willing to risk his life and talk to the cops. He told them the occupants of the armored van were talking to someone in a black Dodge Charger. The driver gunned the Charger and raced across someone's lawn, squealing its tires and drawing attention to it. So, the cops had descriptions of two cars relevant to the investigation of the ATM Solutions robbery, a black Charger, and a black Gran Prix.

A couple of hours later, someone reported to police that a black unoccupied Gran Prix, locked with its engine running, was parked near a car detailing business at 3740 Martin Luther King Drive. That's less than a mile from ATM Solutions. Investigators swarmed on the Gran Prix, unlocked it, processed it and found a .38-caliber pistol on the seat; It was one of the weapons taken from a guard at ATM Solutions.

Patrol officers and detectives continued intensive patrolling around the area (4400 block of Evans) where the armored van was abandoned and recovered. A detective was lazily rolling down Evans when a black Dodge Charger quickly backed out of a driveway and almost collided with the detective car.

The Charger took off; the detective pursued him. Cop detective cars are underpowered staff cars; the detective could have never kept up with the Charger. He did his best to keep the Charger in sight and report to the dispatcher the direction they were both going.

They went south on Grand, east on Olive, and the Charger eventually crashed in the 3400 block of Olive. The driver (John Wesley Jones) got out and ran; it's common procedure for inner city residents to get out and run after crashing their cars, nothing out of the ordinary. He didn't get far, an out of shape beer guzzling detective out ran him, tackled him and wrestled to get him cuffed.

They walked back to the scene of the accident; cops were everywhere, looking and talking. John Wesley Jones was placed in a police cruiser, surly and silent. The detectives opened the trunk of the Charger; $1.4 million was in it.

The FBI figured it was time for action: they cut off the power to the entire 4000 block of Page, cops and agents surrounded the house, tear gas was shot through windows, smashing them.

An FBI military style vehicle sat in front of the house; an FBI agent was seen protruding out of the turret holding a high-powered rifle pointed at the house. They waited for five hours, then sent swat team members inside. There was no one in the house.

The Pontiac Gran-Prix was traced to a Hazelwood, Missouri (beautiful north county) custom car business. The guys who owned the business had loaned the car to, and had helped by doing surveillance of the ATM Solutions building for Rychene Money.

Rychene Money's DNA was found on cigarette butts from inside of the Gran Prix, and inside of the Charger, as well as Money's fingerprints. Money's fingerprints were also found on a revolver found in the Charger.

The stolen cash was in luggage that John Wesley Jones' girlfriend, LaTunya Wright purchased the evening of the robbery, using bills peeled off a large bankroll. Retail clerks talk.

Cops and FBI agents discovered that the robbers had driven the armored van into the garage attached to the rear of Wright's home at 4032 Page, to unload it. Forensic agents from the FBI matched paint from the top of the van to scrapings at the top of the doorway leading into the garage. The van was too tall to get inside without scraping.

The side mirror of the van was missing, knocked off by squeezing into the garage. It was found in a trash container in the alley behind the residence, along with black trash bags consistent with some taken during the holdup.

Cops found John Wesley Jones' Missouri identification card in the house, and bundles of cash in the attic. Bullets were scattered throughout the house, under a stove, on the living room floor and in a dresser.

The FBI brought Latunya Wright in and grilled her; she admitted to taking $600,000 of the ATM Solutions loot to Atlanta and hiding it in a self-storage locker. With John Wesley Jones and Latunya Wright arrested, big problems arose for the numbskull armored car robbers.

Four other women were indicted: Candi Goodson, her mother Cathy Goodson, Yolanda Willis, and Annkesha Welch. They were charged with conspiracy to interfere with commerce by threat or violence. Willis and relatives removed large portions of millions of dollars being stored in a Bellefontaine Neighbors storage facility. She was given the code to the storage facility by Latunya Wright. She used some of the money towards an $8,000 down payment on a Mercedes S430 sedan.

Wright and Candi Goodson went to Willis' home and retrieved $700,000, taking it to Cathy Goodson's north St. Louis County home where they counted and packaged it. Candi Goodson was paid $3,000 Cathy Goodson was paid $50,000. Candi Goodson helped Wright and Welch hide the money in the self-storage facility in Atlanta. The FBI recovered more than $600,000 at the storage facility.

Hassan Johnson was finally nabbed by a federal task force in a home near Tower Grove Park, in the City of St. Louis. He had a wanted in St. Louis County on a previous charge of armed robbery, and was conveyed to the St. Louis County Jail and held.

They had a plan: As Mike Tyson once said, "everybody's got a plan until they're punched in the face."
Each of the bandits was supposed to take a small amount of the cash, and hide the rest. When Larry R. Newman heard that John Wesley Jones violated the deal by driving off with $1.4 million in the trunk of his Charger, he concocted a plan to kidnap Latunya Wright's teenage daughter, and her niece, and hold them for ransom.

He kidnapped them, held them, and then released them unharmed. All the cops and the FBI had to do now was to wait for the robbers to stumble around and continue to make incriminating mistakes. The bozo robbers got girlfriends, friends, and relatives involved in the crime.

The city cops and the FBI patiently waited; the scam, the scheme was imploding. There was a missing man: Aaron H. Johnson; he was arrested. Reychene Money and Wesley Jones pleaded guilty. Reychene was given 19.5 years, Jones, 32-years in prison. Larry R. Newman was waiting his turn to plead.

Greed set in; seven other men, besides the original four, were charged with various related crimes, including splitting up the loot, hiding the loot, extortion and kidnapping. Some of the money was taken to Milwaukee.

Hussein "Vinny" Odeh, pleaded guilty to conspiracy to interfere with commerce with threats of violence and transportation of stolen goods. He admitted that he knew about the robbery beforehand, that he and a co-defendant supplied one of the cars used in the robbery, and that he drove by the building with one of the robbers before the robbery. He also admitted that he had been promised $50,000 for his role, and that he had taken $20,000 to Milwaukee. His co-defendant was Sufian "Sam" Rahman. Odeh is Jordanian, and had immigration issues.

LaTunya Wright's brother, James Wright, became involved simply because he was at his sister's house. He dropped by for a visit; Wesley Jones tossed a $5,000 bundle of cash to him. He accepted it, and helped count and hide the stolen money.

James Wright cooperated with the FBI. His sister pleaded guilty to several charges relating to the robbery and hiding of the cash. She told an acquaintance that her brother sold her out to save his girlfriend and her mother.

Wesley Jones was being held in the Lincoln County Jail, a federally contracted temporary holding facility. He studied the jail for a way to escape; he noticed a flaw in the ceiling in one of the holding rooms; he clawed at the ceiling and tore away dry wall and construction, and crawled his way to freedom.

The FBI wasn't happy about his escape. What these genius crooks don't understand is, that as soon as someone becomes a fugitive, the fed puts a telephone-drop on all of the escapee's friends and relatives, especially concubines, from near and far, past and present.

The feds got a hit; Jones apparently was hiding in Swansea, Illinois, and eastside hamlet about twenty minutes away from St. Louis. U.S. Marshalls (three days after his escape) headed to a house in Swansea, entered, and were searching for Jones; he fell through the ceiling as they were searching the house. They never let you down.

18

In March of 2011, the Sergeant in charge of the Cyber Crime Unit of the St. Metropolitan police Department, wrote a search warrant affidavit, took it to the Circuit Attorney's Office, swore to God that the information within the search warrant affidavit was true, and was granted a warrant to search the residence of Adam Strauss in the 4000 block of Laclede Avenue in the City of St. Louis, Missouri.

But there is always a "what if" factor involved in such searches. Adam was a gun guy; he had dozens of them scattered throughout his residence, and he wore one constantly. "What if", the cyber unit cops kick Adam's door in and he shoots one of them? Or they have to shoot him?

The warrant was, and is, an investigative tool of downtown detective types. It meant they were doing dastardly deeds for their bosses; the ones who sit at their desks and look out of the windows while smoking cigars. They wouldn't waste their time kicking in doors, unless they thought there was something they could pilfer during the raid.

These great detective minds gathered to figure out a way to get Adam out of his abode so they could enter without a stand-off; one of these geniuses decided to contact a trusted friend of Adam's, and to have him lure Adam out of his house.

In the cop/crook business, the first thing a participant learns is: "you have no trusted friends." Smart cops know this fact; play cops do not. So, this trusted friend telephoned Adam and asked him to meet him out in front of his house, in the street in front of 4000 Laclede, with the neighbors watching, and the genius downtown detectives watching in the safety of their take-home detective cars, some with their children's swim toys, and ball gloves in the trunk, a block away, through heavy lenses.

When they observed Adam and his friend in the street, they came on like Chicago Untouchables, screeching their tires and jumping out of their cars, and disarming Adam at gun-point; one of them handcuffed Adam, and they all went into the residence at 4000 Laclede to begin their search.

"What are you looking for?" Adam asks.

"We'll let you know when we find it," one of the detectives replied.

They ransacked the house, and eventually seized several computers, and all of Adam's cell phones, (he had several). They walked out, leaving Adam, his trusted friend, his loyal private secretary, and a couple of hang-on employees wondering what was going on.

Adam wasn't privy to the information in the search warrant affidavit. He wondered what probable cause the detectives had for invading his privacy, cuffing him, and embarrassing him in his home and neighborhood.

Guys like Adam know a lot of people; he hired an attorney, not just any attorney, Scott Rosenblum, the best there is, since Norm London is no longer with us. There was a small blurb in the socialist newspaper about the search warrant executed on Adam, but most of the blurb was chatter about one of his cop employees, Sergeant Robert Ogilvie.

Allegedly, Sergeant Ogilvie arrested a man outside of The Europe Night Club, in the downtown area of the city. The man, Andrew Himless, spent three months in rehabilitation, can't move his left arm, and has trouble walking because of the arrest. Ogilvie and Hi-Tech Security are named as the defendants in the pending lawsuit.

Ogilvie said he observed Himless and a woman in a heated argument outside of the club. Himless appeared to be under the influence of drugs. Ogilvie handcuffed him and sat him on the sidewalk. Himless got up, ran, and his trousers fell to his ankles. He fell, injuring himself.

St. Louis is more of a town than a city. Or, at the most, a small city. Rumors are a big deal in St. Louis, and rumors were flying around town about Adam Strauss and his security company.

One of the rumors sailing around was that someone emailed Adam a pornographic photo; the cyber-crimes unit picked up on it; since they had Adam under scrutiny for being successful, they pounced on him.

His already faltering Hi-Tech Security firm began taking more hits from current, previous, and future contract customers. People of power, the ones who hire security firms, didn't want to be associated with Adam Strauss, or Hi-Tech Security. Adam sold Hi-Tech Security to a long-time employee, Gary Cole. The name of the company was changed. It is now thriving.

The rumors continued. Adam married his loyal secretary. Rumors had it that he married her so she couldn't be compelled to testify against him in a court of law. The case against Adam Strauss lingered, then died. No charges were ever filed against him.

More rumors: Adam was working for the feds, setting people up, snitching himself out of trouble; a confidential informant for the FBI. That's the round peg in the round hole mentality of the City of St. Louis. Cause and effect; an explainable situation why the CWE rich kid wasn't sent to prison. Good old corrupt St. Louis: it never lets you down.

Jimmy Cochran excelled; he is wealthy; he has so much money that his bank wanted to put him on their board of trustees. He drives around town in several expensive cars, one is a vintage Rolls Royce. He has influential friends; politicians, lawyers, FBI Agents, successful businessmen, federal judges (one who incarcerated him twice for bank robbery), news reporters, columnists for the socialist newspaper, The Post-Dispatch.

Jimmy Cochran is a happy man. He is the poster child for criminal rehabilitation. But ask Jimmy a direct question about a previous bank job, or who assisted him in the crime, and he shuts up. He would never snitch on anyone, even if that person set him up for a dive into life-long incarceration. So maybe there is honor among thieves. At least one thief.

As G. Gordon Liddy (Former FBI Agent, lawyer, Nixon Watergate burglar) once said, "Obviously crime pays, or there'd be no crime."

Clay, Bill (United States Congressman) 8,10
Clay, Lacy (United States Congressman) 19
Clark, Raphael (murderer) 57,58,59,81
Clemmons, Reginald (murderer) 209
Cummins, Thomas 209,210

D
Decker, Donna (murder victim) 57,58,59
Decker, Gary (murder victim) 57,58
Dobrowski, Tom (trespasser) 223
Dorrell, John L. III (abduction victim) 77,81,82,118

E
Eidson , George (burglar) 153
Erson, Gregory (detective murdered in Gaslight Square) 23

F
Fabbri, Frank "Tony" (disbarred lawyer, friend to cops) 212,214
Faheen, Sonny (murder victim) 158
Flinn, Brandon (Labor local # 42 boss) 156
Flynn, Ray (Labor local # 42 boss, burglar, murderer) 142,143,149,156
Ford, Dick (television newsman) 228
Ford, Hunter (murderer) 228
Futo, Emory (murderer) 209

G
Georgeff, Steve (police officer shot and mortally wounded by other cops) 10
Giordano, Anthony (Tony G. Gangster, reputed to be the head of the St. Louis Chicago branch of the Mafia) 154
Ghrist, Ray (Homicide detective) 210